"This is a wise and extraordi
Christians can address end-of
loved one's terminal diagnosis, to preparing a runeral, to deal-
ing with grief in the aftermath. Even when explaining complex
medical, ethical, and legal matters, the book is concrete and
accessible. Nancy Duff has written an invaluable guidebook for
helping us approach these difficult topics faithfully and com-
passionately, within our own families, in ministry, with friends
and colleagues—and as we face our own mortality."
—**Victoria Barnett**, general editor,
Dietrich Bonhoeffer works

"I've been waiting for this book since I started using some of
Nancy Duff's articles on death and dying from a Reformed
theological perspective in courses I taught in the 1990s. I know
I'm not alone. Many of us who teach medical ethics from theological perspectives have been waiting for a book that brings
together the wisdom of those who negotiate experiences of
death and dying with those who can provide subtle theological
reflection on those experiences. Speaking on behalf of all of us
who have been waiting, I am glad the book is here and grateful
to Nancy for offering it to us."
—**Mark Douglas**, Professor of Christian Ethics,
Columbia Theological Seminary

"This book is a must-read for individuals and congregations
that want guidance in making faithful decisions around the
end of life. Dr. Duff writes with clarity, conviction, and compassion. In surveying the recent history of the role of physicians in caring for the dying and the decisions of the courts
regarding the end of life, she holds in balance the commitment
to preserve life and the right to live a meaningful life in the face
of death. Her presentation of Christian views of life and death

is succinct and faithful to the witness of Scripture and Christian theology. She provides practical wisdom about advance directives, conversations with physicians, funeral practices, and grieving. Dr. Duff has the gift of expressing her own convictions about making moral decision in the face of death while respecting those who may hold different beliefs."
—**Lewis F. Galloway**, Senior Pastor,
Second Presbyterian Church, Indianapolis, Indiana

"Karl Barth said to a gathering of ministers in 1922, 'It is evident that [people] do not need us to help them live, but seem rather to need us to help them die; for their whole life is lived in the shadow of death.' Every page of *Making Faithful Decisions at the End of Life* offers ministers the practical and ethically sound help we need as we help our congregants walk through the valley of the shadow of death with honesty, theological understanding, and a great trust that 'in life and in death we belong to God.' Duff wrote this with the church in mind, and I commend it not only to ministers but also to adult education committees, book groups, and caregivers."
—**Cynthia A. Jarvis**, minister, The Presbyterian Church of Chestnut Hill, Philadelphia, Pennsylvania

"What is remarkable about this book is the range of end-of-life issues that Nancy Duff addresses with lucidity and wisdom. From crucial theological affirmations about life and death, to the debates over death with dignity and physician-assisted death, to the pastoral and ethical practicalities of advance directives, funerals, and grief, Nancy Duff does not shy away from the hard questions and the urgent realities. I cannot imagine a book more fitting, informative, and helpful for the seminary classroom, the adult study group, the pastor's desk, and anywhere else people of faith seek clarity about choices and convictions at life's outer edge."
—**Thomas G. Long**, Bandy Professor Emeritus of Preaching, Candler School of Theology, Emory University

"Nancy Duff tenders a useful primer on last things and end-of-life concerns, a good text for a necessary conversation."
—**Thomas Lynch**, author of *The Undertaking*

"Professor Duff reviews a wide variety of personal, professional, religious, and social responses to death. She helps readers who wish to live and to die faithfully consider how to hold in tension the call to defend life and the call to seek purpose and meaning in dying. Applications to the professions of medicine and ministry are abundant."
—**Brandt McCabe**, internist and cardiologist,
Princeton, New Jersey

"Dr. Duff challenges believers to consider faithful dying as a continuation of faithful living. With gentle admonition, compassion for the experience of suffering, realistic expectations that are adaptable to individuality, she pushes us all to reflect theologically on a topic most of us would prefer to avoid: our own deaths.

Dr. Duff's gift is her ability to connect the broad sweeps of Christian doctrine to the personal and practical decisions we will all have to make at the end of life. Using a theo-ethical foundation, case studies, insights from her personal experiences, and research in the latest technological/medical advances, Dr. Duff offers the believer concrete options for holding all of life sacred, even as life slips away."
—**Leanne Simmons**, pastor, First Presbyterian Church,
Bismarck, North Dakota

"Professor Duff's book is a rare example of mastery of Christian medical ethics combined with a nuanced understanding of the intricacies of clinical end-of-life complexities. It's a strong recommendation for ethicists in training as well as seasoned professionals."
—**Gabriel Smolarz**, MD MSB, Clinical Assistant Professor of
Medicine, Robert Wood Johnson Medical School,
New Brunswick, New Jersey

"*Making Faithful Decisions at the End of Life* will help clergy, chaplains, families, and congregations navigate the moral and practical complexities involved in terminal illness and death. Readers will garner a wealth of information for further discussion and discernment, including reflections on groundbreaking legal cases, the Georgetown principles, 'death with dignity,' advanced directives, and funeral practices. Throughout this work, Duff develops a Christian contextual ethic based on the tension between resisting and accepting death, and she helps readers to enter into theological reflection on the process of dying well and grieving the dead.

This book is a must for pastoral care classes and congregational book studies, as technology becomes more advanced and the boundaries of life and death more ambivalent. It is a resource that can help pastors better address these tender issues with their congregations and can support those who struggle to make faithful end-of-life decisions. I have been piecing together this subject matter for my students—now I finally have one resource where the issues and their theological implications are expertly presented for future pastors and congregations. This book is an invaluably clear resource on an often-complex issue."

—**Sonia Waters**, Assistant Professor of Pastoral Theology, Princeton Theological Seminary

Making Faithful Decisions
at the End of Life

In gratitude for our friendship
(and I'm so glad you are our
new dean!).

Nancy Duff

Making Faithful Decisions
at the End of Life

Nancy J. Duff

WESTMINSTER
JOHN KNOX PRESS
LOUISVILLE · KENTUCKY

© 2018 Nancy J. Duff

First edition
Published by Westminster John Knox Press
Louisville, Kentucky

18 19 20 21 22 23 24 25 26 27—10 9 8 7 6 5 4 3 2 1

Unless otherwise indicated, Scripture quotations are from the New Revised Standard Version of the Bible, copyright © 1989 by the Division of Christian Education of the National Council of the Churches of Christ in the U.S.A., and are used by permission.

Scripture quotations marked NIV are from The Holy Bible, New International Version. Copyright © 1973, 1978, 1984, 2011 by Biblica, Inc.® Used by permission. All rights reserved worldwide.

Book design by Drew Stevens
Cover design by Marc Whitaker/MTWdesign.net

Library of Congress Cataloging-in-Publication Data

Names: Duff, Nancy J., 1951- author.
Title: Making faithful decisions at the end of life / Nancy J. Duff.
Description: Louisville, KY : Westminster John Knox Press, 2018. |
    Identifiers: LCCN 2018007904 (print) | LCCN 2018024925 (ebook) | ISBN
    9781611648485 (ebk.) | ISBN 9780664263195 (pbk. : alk. paper)
Subjects: LCSH: Death--Religious aspects--Christianity. | Decision
    making—Religious aspects—Christianity.
Classification: LCC BT825 (ebook) | LCC BT825 .D783 2018 (print) | DDC
    236/.1—dc23
LC record available at https://lccn.loc.gov/2018007904

*To Christopher Morse,
my teacher and friend*

Contents

Acknowledgments   ix

Introduction   1

1. Resisting and Accepting Death   6

2. Christian Beliefs about Death   30

3. Assisted Death and Death-with-Dignity Laws   50

4. Physician-Patient Relations and Advance Directives   74

5. Funerals, Burial, and Grief   98

Notes   126

Acknowledgments

I am grateful to everyone who supported me as I wrote this book. I give special thanks to Princeton Theological Seminary for providing me with a sabbatical that made it possible for me to work on this project full time. I am indebted to J. Brandt McCabe, MD, for suggesting twenty-five years ago that I join the ethics committee at Princeton Medical Center and to all the members of that committee for letting me be part of their insightful conversations about end-of-life issues. I will be forever grateful to the Rev. Chunky Young who, less than a year prior to his tragic death in 2016, invited me to be the St. Columba's Lecturer in Johannesburg, South Africa, and, along with the remarkable people of St. Columba's Presbyterian Church, encouraged me to continue my work on the ethics of resisting and accepting death. I am grateful to David Maxwell, acquisitions editor for Westminster John Knox Press, who first suggested I submit a proposal for a book on death and dying. Without his encouragement and his superior skills as an editor, the book would never have come to completion. I thank Julie Tonini, director of production for Westminster John Knox Press, who worked with me throughout the production process. I also thank Frances Purifoy for her careful reading of the text and for applying her significant expertise as a copy editor to my manuscript. Finally, I thank my husband, David Mertz, who was, as always, ever ready with words of encouragement.

Introduction

In 1959 Herman Feifel set out to edit a book on the meaning of death, one of the first of its kind.[1] He wanted to interview dying patients about—of all things—dying. He was, however, met by angry hospital administrators who thought his proposal was cruel and sadistic. Such was the resistance to talking about death almost sixty years ago. We have come a long way since then. Today there are numerous books about dying, including ones by physicians, theologians, CEOs, and, in one case, a children's book author, that are reaching a wide audience, encouraging people to talk about death.

In spite of this impressive increase in popular publications about death, our inability to talk about end-of-life issues has not significantly changed. Many patients do not talk to their physicians or to their families about their wishes at the end of life until they are very close to death—if they ever talk about death at all. As Dudley Clendinen noted a little over a year into living with ALS, "We obsess in this country about how to eat and dress and drink, about finding a job and a mate. About having sex and children. About how to live. But we don't talk about how to die."[2]

There are many reasons people refuse to talk about death. Some people are afraid to die and find that talking about death heightens their fears. A bit of superstition can accompany this fear, making people wonder whether talking about death increases the possibility that death will occur soon. Others may not fear death or even mind talking about it, but they believe (correctly or not) that talking about death will upset their families and friends. And of course, as long as we are healthy, there are always preferable topics of conversation, and once we are ill, talking about death sounds like giving up, which may negatively affect our fight against the disease.

But people's inability to talk about death means that many of them experience dying in a way diametrically opposed to what they actually want. They end up on a ventilator in ICU or endure multiple treatments that prolong their dying without addressing their desire to live well in the last months, weeks, or even days they have left to live. Barbara Moran describes her mother's death in just that manner: "I made peace with her death, but not with her dying. She had four months in the I.C.U., endless and pointless and painful procedures, and final days full of fear and despair. Why is this medicine's default death for so many people?"[3]

Moran does not tell us whether her mother had talked about her end-of-life wishes, but we do know that a tendency among both physicians and patients to avoid talking about death can lead to the kind of death most of us want to avoid. And our inability to talk about death looms large. While many Christian beliefs require us to consider death in the context of Christian faith (the creation story, the crucifixion, the promise of life after death, and death as the last enemy), Christians are no better at talking about their own deaths and what kind of care they want at the end of life than anyone else.

This book encourages Christians to talk about death with their families and friends and with other Christians or people of other faiths or no faith whose perspectives they value. When making faithful decisions at the end of life, Christians need, first, to reflect on death in a highly personal way, considering the kind of end-of-life care they want in light of their Christian beliefs and values. Being able to talk about death includes filling out an advance directive and identifying and talking to a surrogate decision maker as well as indicating preferences regarding one's own funeral. We need to consider seriously how our faith informs our understanding of death and let our preferences regarding end-of-life care be made known to our physicians and family members. Otherwise, we will hand decisions about our care over to others, who may or may not share our values. Christians also need to consider what they believe should constitute public policy or social mores regarding removing life support or whether a doctor can legally prescribe drugs to hasten the death of a terminally ill patient. While we cannot insist that our Christian convictions be made into law or dictate what others believe, we can contribute to the public conversation regarding the appropriate limits of medical intervention in preserving bodily life when death is imminent.

Christians can contribute to (not dictate) the reform of the ethos that defines the medical system so that medical treatments aimed at fighting against death do not preclude the physician and patient admitting when death is imminent and more readily letting go of treatments when they will do more harm than good. As will be clear in what follows, we want physicians to fight against death as the enemy rather than easily or casually accept death and to be committed to saving lives when saving life is possible. But we also want physicians to be able to change goals of care from cure to life-enhancing treatments when death is near.

In researching this project, I frequently drew on three books written by physicians: Atul Gawande's *Being Mortal*, Haider Warraich's *Modern Death*, and Jessica Zitter's *Extreme Measures*. Each of these doctors states that one purpose of writing a book about the medical profession and dying was to help bring about reform. Atul Gawande wonders if better approaches to end-of-life care are so obvious that we simply need to do a better job looking for them.[4] Haider Warraich wrote his book for patients who let him be part of "the most agonizing moments of their lives" and also for himself and other health-care providers so that they can be better equipped to help their patients as they face death.[5] Jessica Zitter hopes to help patients and their families as well as health-care providers find a more humane approach to end-of-life care.[6]

Obviously, these physicians are in a much better position that I am, as a Christian ethicist, to bring about change. Physicians alone, however, should not be required to bear the weight of changing the culture of medicine. All of us need to make our voices heard as we examine our own attitudes about death and challenge the prevailing ethos of medicine so that death is recognized as a condition for which there is, finally, no cure, and life is understood to be more than a beating heart, working kidneys, or lungs expanding and contracting with air flow. It is my hope that this book will help readers contribute to a more humane approach to end-of-life care for themselves personally and also to seek to change our culture by adding an informed voice to public discussions regarding medicine and death.

Chapter 1, "Resisting and Accepting Death," presents court cases that demonstrate problems that arise when physicians or patients believe cure to be the singular goal of medicine. It also describes the Georgetown principles (autonomy, nonmaleficence, beneficence, and justice), which have often guided hospital staff in making moral decisions about end-of-life care. Chapter 2, "Christian Beliefs about Death," sets forth a theological foundation for Christians making faithful decisions at the end of life and presents a Christian contextual ethic that rejects adherence to absolute principles and laws. Chapter 3, "Assisted Death and Death-with-Dignity Laws," examines the pros and cons of death-with-dignity laws according to Christians, disability rights organizations, and physicians. Chapter 4, "Physician-Patient Relations and Advance Directives," describes different types of relationships between physicians and patients and explains the importance and limits of advance directives. It also gives suggestions for how we can talk about death. Chapter 5, "Funerals, Burial, and Grief," compares funeral and mourning practices of the nineteenth century with today, looks at traditional practices for burial and cremation as well as some new options, offers suggestions for what to consider when planning your own funeral, and concludes with reflections on how we live with grief.

After giving a lecture at St. Columba's Presbyterian Church in Johannesburg, South Africa, on end-of-life issues, a woman introduced herself, saying that she was Jewish, she appreciated everything I said, and she agreed with me—not, of course, with my theological convictions that were grounded in the Christian tradition but with my reflections on resisting and accepting death. I hope that even though this book is written from a Christian perspective, it will be of value to readers who are not Christian and that people of different faiths or from a purely secular perspective will be encouraged to talk to one another and learn from one another in both the personal and public arenas of their lives. Public discourse about end-of-life issues can include conversations among people from a variety of traditions. Rather than attempting to find a neutral arena in which various religious and secular narratives are left behind, we may discover areas in which we agree as well as begin to work out how to respect our differences when it comes to the ethics of resisting and accepting death and, for some of us, to making faithful decisions at the end of life.

1

Resisting and Accepting Death

The theological foundation of this book, which is developed in chapter 2, rests on the assertion that the Bible provides two seemingly opposing views of death, both of which need to be embraced by Christians. On the one hand, the Bible says that we are to fight against death as the enemy. On the other hand, it says that we must accept death as an undeniable part of what it means to be mortal human beings and not God. This book rests on the assumption that Christians must hold to both these claims. Hence, when faced with a life-threatening condition, we cannot rely on an absolute principle to preserve life. Rather, we must discern whether it is a situation where death should be fought against or one in which we must accept that this person's time to die has arrived—however untimely that person's death may be.

The medical profession tends to understand death almost exclusively as the enemy to be fought against, even when the fight has reached the point of futility. Bodily life is prolonged as patients are put on what the physician Jessica Zitter calls the "end-of-life conveyor belt." Dying patients are often not told how near death they may be, and treatments are frequently offered that result in prolonged dying rather than a good life in the days, weeks, or months prior to death. And while patients believe that these treatments have some chance at success (and for them, success means cure), health-care providers know otherwise, as Zitter became aware when she was a resident:

> Often in these cases, everyone in that room knew that the patient would never make it out; we may have known it for days prior. And yet we plowed on inserting lines and shouting commands until our higher-ups gave us permission to stop. The assumption was always that more was better.[1]

Of course, we *want* physicians to fight to save our lives. Physicians who readily or casually embraced death would pose a real threat to their patients. But having physicians who continue to treat our bodies or parts of our bodies without looking at the whole person and without acknowledging when further treatment cannot stave off death for any significant amount of time creates unnecessary suffering and robs patients of the possibility of leading a meaningful life as they face death.

The first part of this chapter describes the problems that have arisen from the prevalent collective inability of both physicians and patients to address end-of-life issues in any other way than through relentless and sometimes unreasonable efforts to stave off death as long as possible. The second section describes key court cases regarding patients' rights that initially challenged the prevailing emphasis on cure and allowed patients or their families to discontinue treatment even against the physicians' wishes. It also presents court cases that represent a different dynamic, one in which patients are allowed to demand that all efforts at cure be continued even when physicians believe additional treatments are futile. All these cases focus on the issue of who decides (the physician, the patient and family, or the state) as well as whether there is an absolute moral obligation to preserve life. Finally, the chapter briefly introduces the ethics of resisting and accepting death by describing the often-cited Georgetown principles (autonomy, nonmaleficence, beneficence, and justice). A Christian contextual ethic will be presented in chapter 2.

WHEN CURE IS THE ONLY GOAL

Prior to advances in medicine in the twentieth century, people who were dying were treated like people who were dying. That may seem a simplistic observation, but when the twentieth century saw the introduction of technologies such as mechanical ventilators and CPR (cardiopulmonary resuscitation) and medicine began to cure once-intractable diseases, the goal of medicine and the role of the patient changed dramatically. Now patients with life-threatening illnesses tend to be identified as sick, which of course they are, *rather than* dying, which they may indeed be, and the almost singular goal of care has become cure, *even when cure is no longer possible.* Once given the role of a sick person, a dying patient is expected to comply with every effort of the medical team to fight the disease.[2] Furthermore, fighting the disease means that even talking about death must be avoided by the medical team, the patient, and family members. A good death or, better still, a good life up to the point of death become unattainable because the person with a terminal illness is never recognized (and, therefore, never respected) as someone for whom death is near.

Focusing almost entirely on preserving bodily life can lead to neglecting a person's spiritual, social, and emotional needs. Rather than being surrounded by loved ones and being presented with the opportunity "to make amends, to explain, to bequeath or to apologize,"[3] the dying person is isolated from family and friends—often in ICU (Intensive Care Unit)—unable to take advantage of final opportunities to say things that need to be said. Calling this "the tyranny of survival," Allen Verhey observes that for all the effort to defy death, the opposite of what is intended occurs, for death is allowed an early victory as treatments create as much suffering as the disease itself.[4]

It can be difficult for patients with life-threatening illnesses and their families to determine when to say, "No more." Patients wait until doctors say that they've done all they can, but in reality there is almost always more doctors can do. There are always more drugs, more operations, more radiation treatments or chemotherapy, and then, of course, a feeding tube and a respirator to extend life, or perhaps to extend dying. Jessica Zitter describes this reality in her early days as a physician in ICU:

> And there was always something more to do, something else to try. The protocols that I crammed into my exhausted brain were always about escalating care, designed to guide me through increasing the levels of pharmacologic and technical support. I never even considered that a dying patient might choose comfort as his priority and thus require a protocol to de-escalate the life-prolonging treatments that we steadily heaped on.[5]

Without clear indication from a physician that life-saving treatment has become futile, patients and their families feel caught between *fear* that further treatment will do more harm than good and *hope*, however thin, that the next round of treatment will produce the miracle they are waiting for. Too often they get no clear indication from doctors that further treatment cannot stave off death for long or extend life in any meaningful way. Most physicians say that *they* will not choose medical intervention when they are close to death. Studies have shown that the vast majority of doctors in the United States (almost 90 percent) say that they will avoid aggressive treatment if diagnosed with a terminal illness. But those same doctors are often unable to advise patients to do the same—or even to give them a choice.

The compulsion to treat, of course, is deeply ingrained in doctors' medical training. Jessica Zitter knows that this relentless focus on cure defies that part of the Hippocratic oath recited by medical students that says, "I acknowledge that there is art to medicine as well as science, and warmth, sympathy, and understanding may outweigh the surgeon's knife or the chemist's drug." But having been taught the intricacies of treatment, she says, doctors are never taught how to talk to a patient about dying or to family members when news is bad:

It felt almost cruel to say that the end was approaching, that I thought it unlikely they would survive another hospitalization, that I was concerned they would die on a breathing machine. I didn't have the time nor did I know the words. I didn't have any alternative options to offer besides more treatment.[6]

But sometimes alternative options are what a patient needs. As the physician Atul Gawande claims, "People with serious illness have priorities besides simply prolonging their lives," priorities that include minimizing suffering, interacting with family and friends, being mentally alert, avoiding an overwhelming sense of being a burden, and all the while seeking to achieve "a sense that their life is complete."[7]

Zitter believes her training led her to objectify her patients by using her skills to treat only the body while overlooking the individual human being in front of her. She fears that learning to focus solely on cure—even when cure was no longer possible—diminished the compassion that motivated her to become a doctor to begin with. It was only when a family support team (a precursor to palliative care) inserted itself onto the ICU unit where she worked that Zitter began to change her mind, but even then, it required a monumental effort to overcome her well-ingrained beliefs and turn her attention to more patient-focused care.

Zitter is not, however, suggesting that she or her colleagues in medicine lack compassion. Most of the doctors she knows are compassionate and have the best intentions in caring for their patients. Medicine itself, one might say, fell victim to its own successes, and practitioners have been caught up in an ethos that views death as a disease that can be cured rather than an inevitable event that needs to be acknowledged and discussed, often fought against, but in some circumstances accepted. When the prevailing ethos dictates that further life-saving treatment be pursued even when death is most certainly imminent, the dying patient's physical pain, emotional distress, and other forms of suffering can be ignored. However much compassion may be intended by physicians in their uncompromising fight against death, Zitter knows that this "collective tendency" of doctors (and sometimes patients, as we will see below) to ignore death and focus almost solely on cure "fuels a tremendous amount of suffering."[8]

Nevertheless, even as we criticize medicine, medical training, and doctors themselves for being unable to face the reality of death, we must resist the temptation to demonize medicine. Writing as someone who had benefited from medical treatment for a life-threatening disease, the Christian ethicist Allen Verhey reminds us to be grateful for medicine's ability to resist death:

> We may and should be grateful, of course, for the great advances of medical care in the last century. None of us wants to return to bloodletting and snake oil. We must not neglect the fact that there was a time, not so long ago, when physicians were relatively powerless against the diseases that threaten death and when their ministrations were as likely to kill you as to cure you. The desire for medicine to heal motivated those advances.[9]

Consider the toll in lives lost to cholera, TB, polio, and more recently AIDS when medicine had no effective tools to fight these diseases. Advances in treating heart disease, childhood leukemia, and other forms of cancer are also to be lauded and celebrated.

Unfortunately, in some parts of the world and even in certain parts of our own country, people still die of diseases that now have vaccines, cures, or at least the likelihood of being reduced to chronic conditions for people who have access to medical treatment. Rather than simply rail against medicine for its inability to treat dying patients with honest compassion, we should be grateful and promote access to life-sustaining medical care to every U.S. citizen and every country around the world. But we can also be critical. Being grateful for advances in medicine that can genuinely stave off death and being critical of medicine's tendency to make cure its singular goal even when death is imminent are not mutually exclusive. Despite medicine's great successes, the "failures of those successes," as Verhey says, need to be addressed as well.[10]

It would indeed be wrong to place responsibility for the inability to face death on doctors alone. There is a noticeable movement in the opposite direction involving an increasing number of cases in the United States where doctors *are* ready to stop life-extending treatment while patients, or more often their families, insist that everything be done. Some patients and family members choose to "rage against the dying of the light"[11] against all odds and sometimes against all reason. In one case, even though the patient's body was deteriorating to the point that the odor of death filled the hospital room, the patient's wife insisted that medical treatment continue—until the moment the patient died. This kind of situation puts enormous stress on the medical team, making nurses feel like they are assaulting a human body and being disrespectful of the person who is dying.

Also, doctors often report that when they are able to be honest about a patient's poor prognosis and admit to the patient or family that the next possible treatment will not, in fact, bring the desired results, patients and family members sometimes complain that the doctor has taken away their hope. When Atul Gawande tried to help a patient understand that surgery to remove a tumor could lead to stroke, paralysis, or even death, the patient defiantly replied, "Don't you give up on me. You give me every chance I've got." Gawande describes his own reaction:

> I believed then that Mr. Lazaroff had chosen badly and I still believe this. He chose badly not because of all the dangers but because the operation didn't stand a chance of giving him what he really wanted: his continence, his strength, the life he had previously known. He was pursuing little more than a fantasy at the risk of a prolonged and terrible death—which was precisely what he got.[12]

These Promethean efforts at cure, whether fed by physicians' or patients' inability to face the reality of death, focus too exclusively on death as the enemy and express a tragic idolatry that refuses to accept human mortality.

There are landmark legal cases that reflect this inability of doctors, on the one hand, and patients and their families, on the other, to admit that death is imminent and continued life-sustaining treatments inappropriate. These cases demonstrate that in the arena of both end-of-life care and patients' rights, we have traveled in the proverbial manner of two steps forward and one step back and that in our personal lives, in the world of medicine, in the field of law, and in society as a whole we need to think more carefully and talk more openly about medical treatment at the end of life. Two particular questions will be addressed throughout the summary of these cases: (1) Who decides: physicians, the patient and family members, or the courts? (2) Does human life have absolute value so that medicine and the state have an absolute obligation to preserve life in every case?

COURT CASES

There was a time when patients had virtually no rights regarding medical treatment. Similar to "Father knows best," physicians alone knew what was best and made all significant decisions regarding their patients' care. Most physicians were men, and paternalism tended to define their relationships with patients and their families, who were not allowed to decide when a respirator or feeding tube could be withdrawn or even whether treatment could be rejected altogether.

Some people believe that the patients' rights movement began as early as 1914 with *Schoendorff v. Society of New York Hospital.* After agreeing to be examined under anesthesia, the patient had clearly stated that she did *not* agree to surgery. Nevertheless, she woke up from anesthesia to find that the surgeon had removed a fibroid tumor discovered during the "ether examination." Believing that the surgery resulted in serious complications, including gangrene, she sued the hospital.

Although the judge ruled that the nonprofit hospital could not be held liable, he agreed it was wrong to perform surgery against her will:

> In the case at hand, the wrong complained of is not merely negligence. It is trespass. Every human being of adult years and sound mind has a right to determine what shall be done with his own body; and a surgeon who performs an operation without his patient's consent commits an assault, for which he is liable in damages.[13]

This was certainly a decision on the side of patients' rights. But along with medicine's ability to cure once-fatal diseases, the expertise of physicians and the idea that they alone knew what was best for patients became increasingly ingrained in the ethos of medical care. Fifty-two years after the judge's decision in *Schoendorff,* the case of Karen Ann Quinlan became the first in a series of legal cases in the United States that challenged the assumption that medical decisions were to be left to doctors alone and that preserving bodily life even when no quality of life remained should be the singular goal of medical care.

Karen Ann Quinlan. In April 1975, twenty-one-year-old Karen Ann Quinlan collapsed from an accidental overdose of drugs and alcohol at a bar with friends, who took her home. Once home, in spite of her friends' attempts at mouth-to-mouth resuscitation, she went for two fifteen-minute periods without oxygen. Revived with a respirator by the paramedics and taken to the hospital, it soon became clear that she was in a permanent vegetative state (PVS). She was not brain dead; brain death occurs when there is no discernable activity in any portion of the brain. Had this been the case, she would have been pronounced dead. With PVS the brain stem, which governs basic bodily functions, continues working while the cortex, the upper brain that governs cognition, is severely damaged. Some patients in a permanent vegetative state can breathe on their own, but apart from sporadic instances of spontaneous breathing, Karen Ann Quinlan could not. Hence, a respirator was required to keep air flowing to her lungs and blood to her heart and other organs. No one in a permanent vegetative state can eat or drink with or without assistance; hence, a feeding tube was also required to keep Karen Quinlan's body alive.

With PVS, a patient's body moves through cycles of wake and sleep. Judge Hughes of the New Jersey State Supreme court reported, "In the awake cycle [Karen] blinks, cries out and does things of that sort but is still totally unaware of anyone or anything around her." She existed, he said, "at a primitive reflex level"[14] with no cognitive function at all. All the experts who examined her agreed with this description. Weighing only sixty-five pounds, she was emaciated, and her body, which remained in a rigid fetal-like position, continued to deteriorate.

There are, of course, many disabling conditions that contort a person's body at birth or later in life. The issue here was not about removing a respirator from a newly disabled person. Karen Ann Quinlan had moved into a state of total and permanent lack of consciousness, and her body was deteriorating as well. No treatment would ever in any way improve her condition. And while many people have permanent disabilities that no treatment can reverse, they are not permanently unconscious. They can interact with people around them, know they are loved, and feel happy or sad. Karen Quinlan could do none of these things. She had been reduced to a body that breathed in and out with the assistance of a respirator and a feeding tube. She was not disabled but completely non-abled.

After agonizing over what to do, her devoutly Roman Catholic parents, Joseph and Julia Quinlan, with the full support of their parish priest, requested that their daughter's respirator be removed. Her two physicians, Robert Morse and Arshad Javed (who was a resident serving on the case), refused. When the Quinlans requested that their daughter be transferred, hoping to find a facility that would comply with their request to remove the respirator, her physicians and the hospital refused that as well. The Quinlans went to court, asking that Joseph Quinlan be made his daughter's legal guardian and that he be allowed to dictate the removal of the respirator with no legal consequences resulting for the physicians or the hospital. The New Jersey Superior Court, under Judge Muir, ruled against them. Eventually, the New Jersey Supreme Court granted their request.

At the time of their request, the established ethos of medical care gave almost exclusive right of decision making to physicians. That ethos also included a profound emphasis on prolonging bodily life. Although unofficial actions were sometimes taken by medical staff to allow a patient to die, such as a "slow code" and "judicious neglect," the overwhelming emphasis was on preserving life—no matter what condition that life was in. This ethos is reflected in Judge Muir's report for the lower New Jersey court in his ruling against the Quinlans. The decision to keep or remove the respirator, Judge Muir said, must be left to the treating physician rather than the parents.

> A patient is placed, or places himself, in the care of a physician with the expectation that he (the physician) will do everything in his power, everything that is known to modern medicine, to protect the patient's life. He will do all within his human power to favor life against death.[15]

So extreme was this commitment to preserving even severely diminished life, Dr. Morse's lawyer compared the request to remove the respirator to Nazi atrocities, and Judge Muir compared it to homicide and euthanasia, saying that the state's best interest mandated the preservation of life. The physician's authority to make medical decisions apart from the patient's wishes or the wishes of the de facto surrogate and the state's absolute mandate to preserve physical life were upheld by the New Jersey Superior Court in Judge Muir's decision.

The Quinlans' lawyer, Paul Armstrong, appealed the case to the New Jersey State Supreme Court, which ultimately gave Joseph Quinlan legal custody of his adult daughter and forced the hospital to comply with his request to have the respirator removed. Hence, the two issues under examination here were challenged: physicians did not have the right to be the sole decision makers for medical care, and the state did not have an absolute mandate to preserve bodily life. Karen Ann Quinlan's doctors, however, were undeterred in their commitment to preserving biological life. Drs. Morse and Javed weaned her from the respirator slowly over several months until she was, to everyone's surprise, able to breath on her own. She still required a feeding tube to keep her alive, which the Quinlans were not interested in having removed. In a cruel twist, once their daughter could breathe on her own, they were told that she could no longer stay at the hospital, but no other facility wanted her as a patient either. It took a court order to force a public nursing home to receive her. She remained in that facility just shy of ten years and died in 1985 from complications of pneumonia, for which the Quinlans refused treatment. She was thirty-one years old.

The complex aspects of this case demonstrate the legal and moral confusion over making such decisions. The physicians were afraid of a potential lawsuit, and the hospital, which would not allow a transfer when her parents wanted the respirator removed, was not equipped or presumably obligated to care for her once she could breathe on her own. Other facilities did not want her either. If society believes that life reduced to a permanently unconscious body kept animated by a respirator is worth keeping alive, why did no one want the responsibility of maintaining that body once the respirator was removed, leaving the patient in precisely the same condition as before?

Jon Van, a science writer for the *Chicago Tribune* at the time of Karen Ann Quinlan's death, wrote that the Quinlan case "was unparalleled in its impact on medicine's approach to questions of life and death."[16] Hospital ethics committees, then often referred to as prognosis committees, came into being, and more people understood the importance of making their end-of-life wishes known in writing in what came to be called living wills and then advance directives (the latter including a designation of a surrogate decision maker). Van believed the court's decision successfully reversed the "all-systems-go" technology that fought against death even when the fight had become unreasonable and futile. But for all the significant advances made, subsequent court cases demonstrate that these all-systems-go efforts to fight death at all costs are still well in place, with little clarity regarding the right way forward.

Nancy Cruzan. Fifteen years after the New Jersey State Supreme Court determined that Karen Ann Quinlan's respirator could be removed, the U.S. Supreme Court heard its first so-called "right-to-die case" in *Cruzan v. Director, Missouri Department of Health* in 1990. The key issue at stake was not whether a respirator could be removed from a patient in a permanent vegetative state but whether the family's request to remove a feeding tube could be honored. In spite of the seismic shift in medical care that occurred in the Quinlan decision, events surrounding the Nancy Cruzan case demonstrated that much remained the same after all.

On January 11, 1983, a car accident left twenty-five-year-old Nancy Cruzan in a permanent vegetative state. Four years later, in 1987, her parents' request to remove her feeding tube was denied by the Missouri Rehabilitation Center where their daughter was a patient. In July 1988, a Missouri probate court granted the Cruzan's request to have the feeding tube removed, but four months later in November 1988, the probate court's decision was overturned by the Missouri State Supreme Court. Finally, on June 25, 1990, the U.S. Supreme Court upheld Missouri's right to refuse the Cruzans' request without clear evidence that Nancy Cruzan would not have wanted to live this way. Apart from such evidence, the feeding tube had to remain in place. Rather than a defeat for the Cruzans, the ruling opened the door for presenting such evidence, which they subsequently did in the form of friends testifying that Nancy Cruzan had told them she would never want to be kept alive in a permanent vegetative state. On December 14, 1990, the feeding tube was removed; Nancy Cruzan died twelve days later. She was thirty-three years old. This case, just as with Karen Ann Quinlan, captured the public's eye. Demonstrators stood outside the Supreme Court and then again outside the hospital to protest the removal of the feeding tube while others applauded the decision.

Terri Schiavo. Although no constitutional right to die was recognized in either the Quinlan or the Cruzan case, both cases provided significant legal precedent regarding a patient's or surrogate's right to remove life-sustaining treatment, but they did not, nevertheless, resolve the moral and legal questions. In 2005, thirty years after Karen Ann Quinlan fell into a permanent vegetative state, the case of Terri Schiavo (pronounced "shī-vo") also captured the public's attention. On February 25, 1990, the twenty-seven-year-old collapsed in her Florida home. Her husband, Michael Schiavo, with the support of her parents, Bob and Mary Schindler, sought medical rehabilitation for his wife for eight years. Finally convinced that his wife would never recover, Michael Schiavo, over the strong objections of his in-laws, sought to have his wife's feeding tube removed. The legal battle that ensued between Terri Schiavo's husband and her parents lasted seven years.

During that time, the governor of Florida, Jeb Bush, some members of the U.S. Congress, and the president of the United States, George W. Bush, fought against the withdrawal of the feeding tube. Senator Bill Frist, the Senate majority leader and a heart surgeon, suggested after watching a video of Terri Schiavo that she was not in a permanent vegetative state. Members of her family and their supporters claimed she was in a state of "minimal consciousness," a diagnosis with no basis in fact and one that was ultimately discredited by the autopsy. In spite of objections from political leaders and from parents of children with disabilities who lined the streets in protest, fifteen years after she first collapsed Terri Schiavo's feeding tube was removed for the third and last time. She died thirteen days later on March 31, 2005. She was forty-one years old. The gravestone put in place by her husband reads, "Born: December 3, 1963; Departed this earth: February 25, 1990; At peace: March 31, 2005."

Marlise Muñoz. The starkest evidence of our ongoing confusion over end-of-life issues occurred nine years after Terri Schiavo's death, in 2014, when the body of thirty-three-year-old Marlise Muñoz was kept on what would usually be called "life support." That term, however, is inappropriate because she had been declared dead at John Peter Smith Hospital in Fort Worth, Texas. She was kept on those machines against her husband's and her parents' wishes because she was pregnant. The hospital finally admitted that the baby, who had also been deprived of oxygen for over an hour, was not viable. Keeping a dead body animated to serve as an incubator until a pregnancy can be brought to term is a disturbing situation for some people but not to others. But to keep Marlise Muñoz's body animated when the child was never viable defies all reason and compassion.

Looking at legal decisions from Quinlan to Cruzan to Schiavo to Muñoz, we see that progress has been both significant and faltering in society's ability to allow patients or their surrogates the right to withdraw treatment. There continues, however, to be strong disagreement over whether individuals, physicians, and the state have an absolute obligation to preserve bodily life. Further evidence that medicine and our society as a whole are confused about when to resist and when to accept death is demonstrated by court cases that represent the opposite of physicians' insistence continued care when the family wants it to stop. In these cases, it is the patient or family who insist on continued treatment when the medical team are unanimous that such treatment is futile.

Helga Wanglie and Ruben Betancourt. "She knew where I stood. I have a high regard for the sanctity of human life." Those were the words of Oliver Wanglie regarding his eighty-six-year-old wife, Helga, who was put on a ventilator after her condition was diagnosed as a permanent vegetative state in 1990 at Hennepin County Medical Center in Minneapolis, Minnesota. Her husband acknowledged that the diagnosis was correct. When he and his son and daughter, both in their forties, came to the hospital, they did not talk to their wife and mother because they knew she could not hear them or know they were present. Mr. Wanglie, however, believed that discontinuing care was tantamount to "playing God" and said that his wife had told him she wanted to be kept alive no matter what her condition. He believed that as long as her heart was beating there was life. When the hospital sought to replace Mr. Wanglie with a different surrogate decision maker, the court ruled that Mr. Wanglie had the right to make decisions regarding his wife's care. The court's decision did not address the issue of whether Mr. Wanglie's decision to continue treatment was appropriate. It spoke only to his right to decide on his wife's behalf.

A similar case occurred in *Betancourt v. Trinitas* in New Jersey in 2010, when the daughter of Ruben Betancourt, a patient who was removed from dialysis when the physicians determined he was in a permanent vegetative state, insisted that dialysis and ventilator treatment continue even though the medical team believed this constituted futile care. A New Jersey trial court ruled that the hospital could not withdraw life support without the consent of Betancourt's daughter, again making no determination of whether the daughter's decision was the appropriate one. The hospital appealed the decision, but the patient died before the Appellate Division of the Superior Court of New Jersey made a decision.

Baby K. Two significant cases regarding children, one in 1992 and one more recently in 2013 that is still ongoing, show how the courts have favored patients' rights over the physicians' decision that treatment is futile. Baby K was born with anencephaly in 1992 at Fairfax Hospital in Fairfax, Virginia, and was placed on a ventilator, which the mother refused to have withdrawn even though the doctors advised that Baby K be designated "Do Not Resuscitate" (DNR, often referred to now as DNAR, "Do Not Attempt Resuscitation"). Anencephaly is a condition in which a child is born without the upper brain and only the brain stem exists. It is similar to PVS, but with anencephaly the upper brain is not damaged but missing. (Anencephaly should not be confused with microcephaly, the condition of babies born to mothers who had contracted the Zika virus. These babies have unusually small heads, but a portion of the brain is not missing.) Anencephalic infants are typically treated with comfort care and die within a few days after birth.

Baby K remained on a respirator in Fairfax Hospital for six weeks. Only after she had been weaned off the respirator could she be moved to a pediatric nursing facility nearby. On numerous occasions, however, she returned to the hospital in respiratory distress. When she was six months old, the hospital petitioned for the right to refuse ventilator treatment if she returned and provide palliative care only. Although standard medical practice at the time did not include providing a ventilator for an anencephalic child, the court ruled that the hospital could not refuse to provide such treatment. The court insisted that it was not making a moral judgment but upholding the law, which requires a hospital to stabilize a patient entering the emergency room. The court was relying on the Emergency Medical Treatment and Active Labor Act (EMTALA), but they were upholding the law as it applied to Baby K's respiratory distress while simply ignoring the underlying condition of anencephaly. Baby K died in the hospital on April 5, 1995. She was just under two-and-a-half years old.

Jahi McMath. Perhaps the most disturbing case regarding a patient's family insisting that everything be done for a child is that of Jahi McMath. This case involves a disagreement over how someone is declared dead as well as whether this particular child is indeed dead. In every state in the United States, death can be declared in two ways: when the entire brain, including the brain stem, ceases to function (brain death), or when the heart permanently stops beating (circulatory death). New Jersey is the only state that allows patients' families based on their religious beliefs to insist that death be declared only when the heart stops beating even though the clinical findings of brain death are demonstrated. In such a case, although the person meets the clinical criteria for brain death, death is not declared. Instead, the patient is kept on a ventilator, which allows the heart to continue to beat, while air is artificially pumped into the lungs. In the judgment of most physicians around the country (who accept the definition of brain death) and according to the courts in California, Jahi McMath is dead. Her family disagrees.

On December 9, 2013, Jahi McMath, who was thirteen years old, was admitted to Children's Hospital in Oakland, California, for surgery for sleep apnea (not just a simple tonsillectomy as her parents and the news often reported). Something went terribly wrong after surgery, and she was eventually declared brain dead. Her parents, however, would not accept the opinion of the doctors that their daughter was dead. They not only denied that she was brain dead but also believe that death occurs only when the heart stops beating. The courts agreed with the physicians' pronouncement of brain death, and California does not allow the option of declaring death only with the cessation of heartbeat after brain death has been determined as New Jersey does.

When the body was handed over to Jahi's parents, they transferred her to St. Peter's University Hospital in New Jersey where a tracheostomy was performed and a feeding tube put in place. She remained at St. Peter's for eight months and was then turned over to her mother's care. In their New Jersey apartment, she is kept on a respirator and has twenty-four-hour nursing care covered by Medicaid.[17] Jahi McMath's mother maintains a website on her daughter's behalf, insisting that her daughter is alive and making progress, even claiming she has wielded a pen for drawing, moved her foot on command, and breathed over the ventilator.

The case was further complicated when a physician in California made a medical determination based on viewing a video (much like Senator Bill Frist in the case of Terri Schiavo), declaring that Jahi was not brain dead. This physician's pronouncement may have been influenced by his insistence that the definition of death be based on the heart alone even if the criteria for brain death have been met. In July 2016, the courts once again agreed with multiple doctors who said there had been no change since Jahi McMath was declared brain dead in 2013.

This case is made more complex by the family's belief that the hospital staff did not pay close enough attention to their daughter's bleeding after surgery. They suspected that being African American contributed to what they believe was a lack of appropriate care.[18] This is a complicated and tragic case, but no amount of sympathy for this child's mother can change the fact that Jahi McMath is brain dead, a condition that cannot be reversed. As long as Jahi's body remains on a respirator, her mother can maintain the illusion that her child is improving— an illusion that has sparked support among those who follow her Facebook page but frustration and even anger from those who agree with the physicians and the courts that this child died on December 12, 2013.

These are a few of the cases that made it to court. Reading books authored by physicians like Atul Gawande, Haider Warraich, and Jessica Zitter, one discovers cases that to many of us represent the horrors of the "end-of-life conveyor belt." CPR is performed on patients who are so feeble their bones break from the force of trying to make their heart start beating again.[19] Because dialysis is performed on a dying woman, her loving husband is kept at bay, and she dies hooked up to machines that had no chance of extending her life in any meaningful way and simply made her death worse.[20] A thirty-four-year-old pregnant woman chose to remain in "battle mode" until the very end, even though additional chemo treatments had virtually no chance of extending her life as she continued a steady and painful course toward death.[21]

Lest we think the United States is the only country where there is reason for patients to dread dying more than death itself, Haider Warraich refers to a case from decades ago regarding a British physician who was in extreme pain from stomach cancer in 1968. After surgery removed a blood clot in his lungs that had led him to collapse, his acute pain had become too much to bear, and he asked not to be revived from any future cardiac arrests. He even wrote a note in his own medical chart stating his wishes not to be resuscitated, and he made sure the medical staff knew what he wanted if his heart stopped beating again.

> But even with this knowledge, after two weeks, when he went into cardiac arrest, this time after a large heart attack, he was resuscitated four times that very night. A hole was made in his neck to help him breathe, but his condition after the cardiac arrests was almost subhuman. His brain ceased to function in any reasonable way; he kept having convulsive vomiting and seizures. And yet the staff continued to give him antibiotics and other measures to sustain his life until eventually his heart just stopped.[22]

Apparently, physicians' singular and sometimes unreasonable focus on cure could override the patient's wishes, even when those wishes were crystal clear and even when the patient was himself a physician. The case could just as easily have occurred in the United States in 1968. One hopes that hard-won patients' rights may make it less likely to occur today, but some current cases show that this is not always the case.

These stories present a complex picture of physicians committed to fulfilling their responsibility to keep their patients alive, a responsibility one would not want doctors to take lightly, and of family members who simply cannot let a loved one go, a situation we can well understand. And, then, of course there are worse scenarios, where financial gain may influence a physician to do more than warranted or when family members have ulterior motives in keeping a patient alive or in letting the patient go. It would be cynical—and incorrect—to assert that these latter scenarios are the most common. Each case has its own unique contours, and monetary gain does not routinely drive goals of care, although it does occur. Within this complex human picture, one needs to consider the ethics of resisting and accepting death. No simplistic approach, such as an absolute adherence to extending bodily life or a casual acceptance of death as inevitable will suffice when making decisions about end-of-life care.

THE GEORGETOWN PRINCIPLES

Haider Warraich says that there were no villains in the Quinlan case, and Judge Muir described Karen Ann Quinlan's physician, Dr. Morse, as "a man who demonstrated strong empathy and compassion."[23] It would certainly not be fair or wise to identify villains in such a complicated case from so many decades ago, but one could conclude that Dr. Morse's compassion was diminished by making preservation of the body his singular goal of care. In spite of being presented with a sixty-five-pound body that functioned only at the level of reflex due to irreversible brain damage and in spite of acknowledging that Karen Ann Quinlan had no awareness of anything or anyone around her and no chance at recovery, Dr. Morse refused to consider quality of life as he denied the request to withdraw the respirator and later as he slowly weaned her from it.

It is difficult not to assess Dr. Morse's decision as irrational, if not cruel. But as we have seen from a variety of court cases, some patients and their families also seek to follow an absolute mandate to preserve bodily life. Perhaps rather than vilify physicians or patients and their families, one can identify as villainous the adherence to an absolute mandate to preserve life, even when life has been reduced to nothing more than an animated body sustained by machines. Equally important, of course, is that one cannot turn to a casual acceptance of death as a foil to overtreatment at the end of life.

Knowing when to resist and when to accept death presents a moral and existential dilemma that is not easily resolved. Chapter 2 includes a description of contextual ethics from a Christian perspective that calls into question any approach to ethics that tries to apply clear, formulaic principles that cannot take into account an individual's suffering or adequately address what Paul Lehmann liked to call "the daily living of human life." This ethic is based on biblical and theological convictions for Christians to consider when addressing end-of-life issues for themselves personally and when contributing to the public discussion from their own particular religious perspective with no presumption of imposing Christian views on everyone else. The remainder of this chapter will look at the nonreligious Georgetown principles that are often invoked in hospitals when physicians and other personnel are contemplating a moral dilemma regarding treatment.

In a highly influential book, Tom L. Beauchamp and James F. Childress presented four principles for biomedical ethics.[24] Referred to as the Georgetown principles because the authors lived in Georgetown, Virginia, these four principles have become widely used in medical ethics, even by those who are unaware of who wrote them or what they were originally called. Sometimes they are presented with slight alterations, but in their original and most typical form they are autonomy, nonmaleficence, beneficence, and justice.

The principle of autonomy respects a patient's right to make informed decisions regarding medical treatment. Nonmaleficence can be summarized in one of the best-known dictums in medical ethics: "Above all, do no harm." Beneficence requires positive action that promotes the patient's welfare, in contrast to nonmaleficence, which demands only that one refrain from doing harm. The principle of justice requires fair distribution of medical resources even in specific cases so that treating one patient cannot lead to the neglect of others. No hierarchy was intended in this list of principles. Physicians and other members of staff making moral decisions regarding medical care are expected to balance the four principles in each particular case. Eventually, however, patient autonomy took the lead and has sometimes become an absolute principle that outweighs the other three.

Problems arise if one ignores the delicate balance Beauchamp and Childress were seeking to achieve and instead allows any of them to be given absolute status. As we have seen, autonomy, when made absolute, results in patients being given the right to demand inappropriate end-of-life treatments, which can in fact contradict the principles of justice if resources are used for inappropriate care for one patient at the expense of another patient's needs. When nonmaleficence is interpreted as an absolute obligation to keep a body alive at all costs, suffering can ensue for the patient and the patient's family as well. The physician and medical ethicist Edmund Pellegrino argues that these principles are problematic even if the balance is achieved because they are

> too abstract, too rationalistic, and too removed from the psychological milieu in which moral choices are actually made; principles ignore a person's character, life story, cultural background, and gender. They imply a technical perfection in moral decisions that is frustrated by the psychological uniqueness of each moral agent or act.[25]

In other words, Pellegrino claims that even when one follows the right principles, one can fail to do the responsible thing in relation to *this* particular person.

In spite of these objections, the four Georgetown principles have proven to be useful tools for helping people sort out what is at stake when making a decision about a moral dilemma involving care. Taking Pellegrino's concerns into account, the principles can actually be used *alongside* a compassionate understanding of a patient's personal and social history. They cannot, of course, be expected to resolve moral issues by providing a consensus among caregivers. One person might believe that doing no harm means doing everything possible to keep a patient alive while another might insist that ongoing treatment that will not bring the person a life worth living is doing the patient harm. But even if the four principles do not bring about consensus, they can help clarify various aspects of a complex situation.

These principles do not constitute a specifically Christian ethic. Christians should, however, be aware of the Georgetown principles, their potential use by hospital personnel, and even their potential strengths as Christians ponder these complicated issues. But to make faithful decisions at the end of life, Christians also need to turn to moral decision making based on Christian faith. Chapter 2 will propose that such moral decision making forswears adherence to absolute principles and laws and seeks to discern the will of God in each particular situation. This presentation of a Christian contextual ethic is not meant to suggest that Christians should force their faith or religious beliefs on others, but it affirms that public discussion among people of different faiths or no faith should reflect particular beliefs and identify areas of agreement and disagreement rather than seek some nonexistent neutral ground.

QUESTIONS FOR REFLECTION

1. Are physicians being compassionate when they insist that everything be done to preserve someone's life? How else could physicians show compassion consistent with their professional obligations?
2. Should there be a limit on a patient's or family's demands that everything be done when the medical team believes that further treatment would be futile?
3. Should doctors be honest about a patient's poor prognosis even when the patient and the family clearly don't want to hear bad news?
4. Should someone other than a doctor be present to deliver a poor prognosis?
5. Is it possible to balance the Georgetown principles (autonomy, nonmaleficence, beneficence, and justice), or will one always take priority over the others?

2

Christian Beliefs about Death

In the Middle Ages, the church produced what we might call self-help books that aimed to assist Christians in preparing for death. One of the best known was *Ars Moriendi* [The Art of Dying] produced in 1450. The book included woodcuts, one of which depicted five temptations in the form of demons surrounding the dying person: losing faith, giving way to despair, impatience, pride, and avarice (greed). Images of virtues represented by angels surrounding the bedside of a dying person were presented as antidotes for these temptations: faith, hope, love, patience, humility, and letting go. As Allen Verhey points out, there are theological problems with some of the material presented in *Ars Moriendi*. For instance, devotion to this life is considered a form of greed, an idea that denies the goodness of bodily life and is more consistent with the notion of the eternal soul that sheds insignificant bodily existence than with the Christian affirmation of the bodily resurrection. But the overall goal of the whole *Ars Moriendi* genre is commendable as the church sought to prepare Christians for death in the context of faith.[1]

A contemporary self-help pamphlet about how to die would be unwelcome by most people today. But the church has a role to play in providing a space where its members can talk about death and in encouraging them to consider the affirmations of the faith as they contemplate—and prepare for—their own deaths and the deaths of those they love. This does not call for the church to reinvent the wheel. The church has a long history of hospitality toward those who are in need, with Matthew 25 leading the way: "'Truly I tell you, whatever you did for one of the least of these brothers and sisters of mine, you did for me'" (Matt. 25:40, NIV). Dying patients may not start out as the least of the brothers and sisters, but the combination of disease and treatment can separate them from their sense of self and from their community and may even make them feel alienated from God. Not only is the church called to be present at such a time, it can help prepare its members to face death long before terminal illness has begun to take its toll.

Chapter 1 described problems that arise when cure is considered the almost singular goal of medicine. It also suggested that absolute moral laws are inadequate for addressing the complexities of life and of dying. This chapter will examine five fundamental Christian beliefs regarding death that may help Christians negotiate these complexities as they seek to navigate conversations and make faithful decisions about the end of life:

— Death is the enemy to be resisted, *and* death must be accepted as part of what it means to be mortal human beings.
— The contextual nature of Christian ethics forswears absolute rules and principles when making decisions about end-of-life care.
— Even when facing death, Christians insist on the importance of bodily life as expressed in creation, incarnation, and resurrection while at the same time insisting that life cannot be reduced to bodily existence.
— The doctrine of vocation affirms that our lives have purpose even as we face death.
— Praying for a miracle shouldn't prevent us from faithfully preparing for death.

All these affirmations are made in light of the first question and its answer in the Heidelberg Catechism: "What is your only comfort, in life and in death?" with the response "That I am not my own, but belong—body and soul, in life and in death—to my faithful Savior, Jesus Christ."[2]

RESISTING AND ACCEPTING DEATH

The Bible offers two seemingly contradictory affirmations regarding death: Death is the enemy to be fought against, *and* death must be accepted as part of what it means to be mortal human beings. Rather than choose between these two affirmations, Christians need to hold both in tension.

Death is the enemy to be fought against. The Bible teaches that death is not only viewed as the cessation of life but also as the enemy that stands for all the destructive powers of the world that cause pain and suffering and that damage life. Death takes its place among the "powers and principalities" and is thus understood as something more than just an individual's loss of life. Paul tells us that death is a power that has dominion over the earth, is an ally of sin, and is the last enemy (1 Cor. 15:26 and Rom. 6:23). Death for Christians is not simply a natural part of life, a friend, or a transition from one stage of life to another, but the enemy. Tom Long refers to this biblical understanding as "capital-*D* death," saying that death is a "mythic force" and the enemy of everything God wills:

> Death in this form is out to steal life from human beings, but it does not stop with individuals. Death wants to capture territory, to possess principalities. It desires to dehumanize all institutions, poison all relationships, set people against people in warfare, replace all love with hate, transform all words of hope into blasphemy, to fuel the fires of distrust, to lead people to the depths of despair, to shatter all attempts to build community, and to make a mockery of God, faith, and the gift of life. It is "the pestilence that stalks in darkness" and "the destruction that wastes at noonday" (Ps. 91:6).[3]

This apocalyptic and cosmic understanding of death is not unrelated to the death of an individual. Capital *D*-death can snatch the lives of children, and it can deplete the life of a young or elderly person long before the last breath is taken. It is the death that Christ defeated on the cross, but while Christ's victory over death has the last word, death still has destructive force in this world.

Death must be accepted as part of what it means to be mortal. In addition to teaching that death is the enemy to be fought against, the Bible also says that we need to accept humanity's finitude. Adam and Eve were never created to be immortal. In the story of the fall, we hear God say that Adam and Eve must be driven out of the garden lest they eat from the Tree of Life and become like the heavenly hosts—in other words, lest they become immortal (Gen. 3:22–23). That we are mortal, finite beings marks a significant difference between ourselves and God. The Bible teaches us that to cling too tenaciously to life in this world, denying the reality of death, is a form of idolatry. Tom Long refers to this second biblical view as "small-*d* death," which simply recognizes the mortality of human beings: "We have a life span, short or long; we are born, we live, we die. This form of death marks us off as human and not divine."[4]

Acknowledging our mortality, however, should not be mistaken for an idea that has crept into the Christian perspective on death that emphasizes the claim, somewhat matter-of-factly made as if easily accepted, that "death is natural." As Allen Verhey points out, the "Death is natural" mantra can mean different things to those who use it. Some people simply mean that death is a part of life that we as humans share with all living things: "At the end of life, people die. What could be more 'natural' than that?"[5] Others use the claim that death is natural not only to remind us that death is a biological event that will be experienced by us all but also to insist that death provides meaning as a natural process of growth. Hence, Elisabeth Kübler-Ross edited a book titled *Death: The Final Stage of Growth.*[6] The third meaning of the "Death is natural" mantra could be likened to the "circle of life" philosophy set forth in

Disney's movie *The Lion King*. Death is understood as one of the natural rhythms of nature; birth and death are similar to the cycle of the seasons from spring to winter and eventually back to spring. The image of a caterpillar becoming a butterfly is often used to indicate that death is simply a transition from one form of life to another.[7]

People who use the refrain "Death is natural" are seeking to increase our awareness of death and make it easier—more natural—for us to talk about our wishes at the end of life—a worthy goal—but each of the interpretations of the "Death is natural" refrain raises problems that make it difficult to reach this goal. First, to claim that death is a part of life and thus inevitable can be readily accepted by most people as a universal truth, but as Verhey points out, accepting the more biographical claim "*I* am going to die" is much more difficult. Claiming that death is natural does not tend to make it easier for people to discuss the end of their own particular life's story, which may not feel natural at all.[8] The second claim—that death marks a final moment of growth—is odd at best, since death actually involves the end of life, when growth is no longer possible.[9] The third interpretation—that death puts us in line with the harmony of nature—is exposed as problematic by Tom Long, who offers a disturbing example from a denominational study that concluded,

> Death for an older person should be a beautiful event. There is beauty in birth, growth, fullness of life and then, equally so, in the tapering off and final end. There are analogies all about us. What is more beautiful than the spring budding of small leaves, then the fully-leaved tree in summer; and then in the beautiful brightly colored autumn leaves gliding gracefully to the ground? So it is with humans.[10]

Long interprets this "death-embracing language" as an example of how the church sometimes loses sight of its own "bold and clear-eyed theology" regarding death.[11] Personally, I can't help but wonder what the study means by "older person" and how anyone who falls into that category wouldn't be insulted.

Having lived past sixty-five, am I now to be compared to an autumn tree, and have I become someone who should embrace my own death as a beautiful thing? Even when my ninety-year-old mother passed away with advanced Alzheimer's, knowing that her time to die had arrived and that she was ready to die, it should not even need to be said that her death was far more significant than a leaf gliding from a tree. And there was very little that was beautiful "in the tapering off and final end" of her life.

Tom Long points out that insisting that death is simply a natural part of the ebb and flow of life can lead to an unchristian sentimentality, and he cites as an example Nancy Byrd Turner's poem "Death Is a Door," which has made its way into some Christian funerals. The poem claims that "death is only an old door set in a garden wall." "Willing and weary" feet walk up to that door, because "there is nothing to trouble any heart" and "nothing to hurt at all."[12] This poem offers a ready answer to Paul's rhetorical question "'Where O death is your victory? Where, O death, is your sting?'" (1 Cor. 15:55), but the answer stems from the notion that there isn't anything ugly or destructive about death to begin with. Death is not the enemy. Death is natural.

Long also considers another popular poem, this one written by Mary Elizabeth Frye, that has found its way into some Christian funerals and that not only denies that death is the enemy but also denies death itself. The poem begins, "Do not stand at my grave and weep; I am not there. I do not sleep."[13] Concluding with the bold claim "I did not die," the person, who has in reality died, not only can be found in nature but also actually *is* various aspects of nature: the winds that blow, the sunlight on grain, and birds in flight. According to this philosophy, the circle of life is indeed complete. No one dies; they just reappear as wind and rain and sunlight on snow. This sentimentality does not represent the Christian view of death as presented in the Bible. And on a personal note, my mother is not the wind. She did indeed die, and we did, and on occasion still do, stand at her grave and weep.

Consistent with the "Death is natural" mantra, the Bible acknowledges human mortality. There is "a time to be born, and a time to die" (Eccl. 3:2). Isaiah tells us,

> All people are grass,
>> their constancy is like the flower of the field.
>
> The grass withers, the flower fades
>> when the breath of the Lord blows upon it;
>> surely the people are grass."
>
> (Isa. 40:6–7)

God declares, "'My spirit shall not abide in mortals forever, for they are flesh" (Gen. 6:3). The Bible insists that we accept the mortality that is ours by virtue of being created human beings and not gods. Nevertheless, quite contrary to the idea that death is natural, the Bible never says that death is beautiful. There may be beautiful moments when people show courage and even humor in the face of death and when someone is able to extend final expressions of love, forgiveness, and reconciliation. Even simply a peaceful fading away can include a certain kind of profound beauty, but it is not the same as saying that death itself is beautiful. And it is certainly not the same as comparing the death of an individual human being, whose life's story has come to an end, with a leaf falling from a tree.

Human beings may indeed be called to live within the rhythm of nature, acknowledging our connection with all finite creation, but for Christians death always remains *also* the enemy. In fact, the most significant difference between the Bible's insistence that we accept our mortality and the "Death is natural" mantra is that the latter leaves no room for this "*also*." Christians, in contrast, accept death as part of human mortality, and we *also* believe that death is the enemy. We hold these two affirmations about death in tension as we acknowledge that in life and in death we belong to God. Knowing that the grass withers and the flower fades and that we are like the grass can be terrifying, but Isaiah uses this observation to make the reassuring claim that "the word of our God will stand forever" (Isa. 40:8). The Bible does not teach us to find beauty and comfort in death itself, and certainly not in nature, but in the constancy and grace of God.

We affirm the constancy and grace of God by holding both views of death at a funeral, but, as Tom Long points out, depending on the situation, the pastor may emphasize one over the other:

> If we thunder out only denunciations of death the final enemy, we may obscure the fact that death, biological death, can sometimes come as a friend, ending pain and halting the merciless fall of sufferers into despair. . . . On the other hand, if we forget about Death's bloody saber and focus only on death as a part of the natural flow of life, we can be seduced into bland and finally unchristian bromides about death.[14]

As the author of Ecclesiastes knew, there is "a time to be born and a time to die" (Eccl. 3:2). There is a time to hold on and a time to let go.

THE CONTEXTUAL CHARACTER
OF CHRISTIAN ETHICS

Discerning when to hold on and when to let go leads to a clear decision in some situations but an agonizing one in others. We saw in chapter 1 that the overriding ethos of medicine has often been informed by two interlocking notions. First, death is the enemy that physicians must fight against almost until patients take their last breath. Second, augmenting the absolute obligation to preserve bodily life is the notion that life has absolute value. Judge Muir represented these two intertwining ideas when in the case of Karen Ann Quinlan he said that a physician is expected to "do all within his human power to favor life against death." While this may sound like a responsible claim when made in a general way, it is alarming when one considers that he said this in a situation where life had been diminished to an emaciated and rigid body sustained by artificial means and when he knew the patient would never again have any awareness of the world around her.

Some Christians seek to make faithful decisions at the end of life based on these same two interconnected ideas: (1) there is an unconditional obligation to preserve life (2) because life has absolute value. The unqualified obligation to preserve life often arises from a particular way of interpreting the sixth commandment: "Thou shalt not kill" (Exod. 20:13 KJV). For Christians who believe this is an absolute command always to be followed in the same way in each situation, the decision to withdraw treatment is rarely made until patients are very close to taking their last breath. These Christians often invoke the refrain "God gives life; God takes life away" (drawing on such texts as Job 1:21, Deut. 32:39, and 1 Sam. 2:6), insisting that withdrawing life-sustaining treatment is the same as taking life, which only God can do. Sometimes believing that we must adhere to an absolute command to preserve life is accompanied by the desire to give God time to bring about a miracle, although one may wonder why God's miracle depends on the continuation of medical intervention.

A Christian contextual ethic (not to be confused with a utilitarian "situation ethic") recognizes that absolute laws, principles, or commands cannot adequately address the complexities of human life. Even the commandment "Thou shalt not kill" cannot be applied in the same way to every situation. Believing that we are *always* to fight against death and *never* accept that death is near relieves us of looking at the real human being who is placed before us. We need instead to discern God's will for this particular person at this particular time and determine whether we should fight against death as the enemy or accept that this person's time to die has arrived. It may, of course, be a horrible time for the individual to die, but accepting that death is near and changing goals of care from cure to comfort may be what is required to preserve life while life lasts, allowing the person to have a good life up to the point of death and then to have as good a death as possible.

"Thou shalt not kill" is not an absolute law to be applied to various situations but a way of life that calls us to fight against death when the fight can make a difference and to exhibit God's grace and comfort when the fight is over and death is near. To forswear the absolute character of divine commands does not mean that we ignore them or seek to manipulate them to suit our own whims. Rather, it means that we shift our focus from *keeping the commandments* to *obeying the living God* who gives the commandments.

Those who believe in an absolute command to preserve life often also believe that respect for life forms the fundamental principle of ethics and that life itself constitutes the highest good. For them, all moral principles, laws, and virtues are subordinate to the absolute value of life itself. This claim, however, is not consistent with Christian faith. In fact, to suggest that life has supreme value is a form of idolatry. Only God is the highest good. This does not mean that life becomes insignificant or expendable. One does not center one's life around God at the *expense* of human life. We don't, however, worship life; we honor it. And sometimes we are called to honor life by recognizing that a person is, in fact, dying and the time has arrived to stop fighting against death.

We need to understand, however, that some Christians' motivation for refusing to withdraw treatment is based on deep-seated mistrust of the medical profession. Historically, African Americans in particular have been treated in such a way that trust in the medical profession has been severely, and one can only hope not irredeemably, damaged. Decades of segregation meant lack of access to the best medical care primarily because enrollment into medical school for African Americans was limited to a few black medical schools and because African American patients were often barred from seeing white doctors. African American trust in the medical system was also seriously eroded by the forty-year-long Tuskegee experiment (1932–72), which was conducted without the informed consent of the unknowing participants.[15] Because the researchers wanted to monitor the natural progress of syphilis, they didn't provide genuine medical treatment for the black men who participated. Instead, the men were given free medical exams, free meals, and burial insurance. Even when penicillin was shown to address the disease, it was not offered to the study participants because researchers knew that it was their last chance to trace the disease without medical intervention.

Even now that segregation has ended and the number of African American physicians has increased, the percentage of African American doctors has yet to match the percentage of African Americans in relation to the general population.[16] And even though protocols are in place to protect subjects of medical research from abuse, racism in our culture along with the history of mistreatment feeds the legacy of mistrust, and African Americans are less likely to volunteer as research subjects than whites. Also, as a result of this mistrust, African Americans are more likely to check "Do everything" on their advance directives than whites and may be highly suspicious of the motivations behind a medical team who suggests withdrawing life support or moving to hospice care. The commitment to doing everything to stave off death until the last breath is taken may also be augmented by Christian beliefs and waiting for a miracle, but mistrust of the medical system has an enormous impact on making faithful decisions at the end of life for many African Americans. Any disagreements we may have with decisions made need to be set within the context of the legacy of abuse and neglect and the resulting mistrust of the medical system.

Other groups who continue to be the targets of racism or other forms of discrimination, such as that experienced by people with disabilities, may also fall more firmly on the side of resisting death than accepting it in light of their mistrust of the medical profession. We may disagree with the individual decisions of people who fall within these groups, but their decisions may point to a systemic problem that needs to be more rigorously addressed even as some of us hold that there are situations where the time to hold on has past and the time to let go has arrived. Furthermore, their suspicion reminds us that we must never let go of life because of any utilitarian sense that an individual no longer has value or that a person's life is expendable and can easily be let go. Only respect for a person who is now facing death should lead us to ask whether it is time to accept death—never a determination that this person's life is past the point of being valuable.

THE SIGNIFICANCE OF BODILY LIFE

Seeking to discern when to hold on and when to let go from a Christian perspective does not allow for a casual attitude about death being natural, as argued above. Nor do Christians hold that this bodily life is insignificant and easily dismissed when we face death. The poems mentioned above that suggest death is nothing more than a garden wall or that we do not die but live on as elements of nature inadvertently dismiss the significance of bodily life, suggesting that the body is merely a shell the soul leaves behind as it transitions into a new state of being. The Christian faith stands against this perspective, affirming that we are created, redeemed, and resurrected as *embodied* individuals. In Christian faith, a human person cannot be reduced to bodily existence, but the body is, nevertheless, highly significant.

When my daughter was very young, I talked to her about the death of a close family member. Seeking to reassure her that when a body is buried after someone dies, no one is being buried alive, I told her that when we die, God takes that part of us that God loves the most to heaven. She began to ask a series of questions: Does God love our hair? Does God love our skin? Does God love our bones? I realized that my reassurances were much more in line with the notion of an eternal soul that sheds the insignificant body at death than the Christian understanding of bodily resurrection represented in her questions. The Christian faith does not believe in an eternal soul that resides in an inconsequential shell that one assumes at birth and from which one is liberated at death. The Christian faith affirms the significance of bodily life in beliefs about creation, incarnation, and resurrection.

The significance of bodily life is affirmed by Christian beliefs about *creation*. Genesis tells us that God created the world and called it good. The physical things of this world—the sun and moon and skies, the fish of the sea and the birds of the air, the animals, and most certainly human beings—are declared good in their finite physical forms: "God saw everything that he had made, and indeed, it was very good" (Gen. 1:31). The significance of bodily life is also affirmed in the Christian understanding of the *incarnation*. God did not shun bodily life or seek only to save the human soul. God was incarnate in this world of "time and space and things," as Paul Lehmann liked to say.[17] The importance of the physical body is affirmed yet again by the Christian belief in *bodily resurrection* as was reflected in my young daughter's questions far more clearly than in my reassurances. Fundamental to the Christian faith is the empty tomb of Easter. There was no life and no potential for resurrection in the human Jesus' dead body taken down from the cross. Just as God created the world from nothing, God resurrected Jesus from the nothingness of death. Christians know that our physical bodies disintegrate, but Christian faith affirms that we as distinct individuals will experience new life and recognizable, albeit, resurrected bodies even as our earthly bodies will return to dust.

There are times when the church errs from its own teachings by forswearing things pertaining to the body, especially things that have to do with human passion and sexuality. But the doctrines of creation, incarnation, and resurrection affirm the goodness of bodily existence: God created us as both body and soul and saves us as whole human beings, including both our physical and spiritual selves.

Even as the Bible affirms the significance of the body, it also knows that our bodies are frail. The grass withers, Isaiah says: "Surely the people are grass" (Isa. 40:7). Even the strongest body withers and sometimes literally wastes away under the onslaught of cancer or other life-threatening diseases. And sometimes the mind begins to fade away as well. Although physicians' commitment to keeping death at bay is consistent with the Christian belief that death is the enemy and bodily life is worth preserving, the Christian understanding of the human person has never reduced human beings to bodily existence, and medicine shouldn't either. Human beings are more than animated bodies that breathe in and out, with or without the use of a respirator. This is not to say that lives cease to have value when bodies are broken, but only that the Christian tradition values the whole human being, body and soul.

VOCATION

The doctrine of vocation, which affirms that each human being at every stage of life has purpose, can also guide us as we die or when we are present with someone else who is dying, and it can help us make faithful decisions at the end of life. In its most fundamental meaning the doctrine of vocation claims that God calls each of us into being for a divinely appointed purpose. John Calvin captured this affirmation in his reflections on Psalm 22:9:

> Although it is by the operation of natural causes that infants come into the world . . . yet therein the wonderful providence of God shines forth. This miracle, it is true, because of its ordinary occurrence, is made less account of by us. But if ingratitude did not put upon our eyes the veil of stupidity we would be ravished with admiration at every childbirth in the world.[18]

As God calls us into being, each life has meaning and purpose at birth. And so, too, throughout life, our lives have purpose even if we have lost our way. This means we can say to one another, "Your life matters. Your life matters where you are and who you are right now."

This affirmation should not be misunderstood to mean that

there is a purpose to every place and circumstance in which we find ourselves or to everything that happens around us or to us. The popular refrain "Everything happens for a reason" is not being affirmed here. Rather, the doctrine of vocation affirms that no matter where we are or what has happened to us, God has a purpose for us. Part of God's purpose may include our seeking to leave the situation in which we find ourselves, if possible. But those circumstances, however demeaning or painful, cannot diminish our value in the sight of God.

This affirmation that each life has purpose and meaning includes someone who is dying. When one's physical life is diminished by terminal illness so that dependence on others is increasingly necessary, when a decision is made to withdraw treatment from a dying person, or even if a person decides to take advantage of an aid-in-dying law, none of those things mean the individual's life no longer has purpose and value. No crass utilitarian thought is at work whereby one chooses not to try to preserve the life of an individual because that life is no longer productive, valued, or loved and so has become expendable. Rather, purpose and meaning are now sought in the life of a dying person, who deserves to be treated with respect *as someone who is dying*. And there may come a time when one's purpose includes seeking a good death.

The Christian understanding of vocation also says that we are called to glorify God in all that we do. Glorifying God can be understood by looking at the three parts of the commandment in Matthew 22:37–39: (1) "Love the Lord your God with all your heart, and with all your soul, and with all your mind" and (2) ". . . love your neighbor" (3) "as yourself." Is it possible as we face death that we can trust in God to whom we belong, not to fix all that literally ails us but to be ever present, affirming that whatever tedium, inconvenience, disability, or pain that is brought on by illness, we can trust that we are loved by God? Is it possible as we face death that we can love our neighbors and trust in them to take on tasks that we can no longer perform, to remind us that the purpose of our lives continues even as what we can do and what we have to endure shifts, sometimes daily? Is it possible that even as we face death, even in whatever diminished state our illness has created, we can love ourselves as children of God? These questions are not intended to suggest expectations or demands placed on us as we die. Instead, the possibility of affirmative answers should be understood as a blessing.

These questions also lead to a third aspect of vocation, which addresses those who are called to be present with those who are dying: we are to help create a space where it is possible for others to glorify God. Christians are called to help create such a space for those who are close to death, reminding them that they are loved by God and that their lives are no less meaningful now that life is coming to an end. It can be extremely difficult at times for individuals to find continued purpose as both disease and treatment redefine what they are able to do. What it means to be a parent or a friend may shift dramatically as tasks once performed with ease are now impossible. It may require a community of faithful people to encourage those who are facing a terminal illness to accept their value in this changing context.

We need, however, to remember that being called to glorify God as we face death is *not* a demand but a promise and a blessing. Without judgment or condemnation, we recognize that for some Christians glorifying God as they die can become challenging and sometimes even impossible. Physical and emotional pain, disappointment, fear, and a sense of being overwhelmed by life's ending may make it impossible for some people to die a good death with a strong faith that prevents them from falling into despair. This is when it is especially important to remember that what is being affirmed by the Christian understanding of vocation is that we *may* glorify God as we die—not that we *must*. The point is not to instill guilt in those who cannot find the resources to maintain faith with no edge of doubt, anger, or fear. Sometimes the terminally ill cannot overcome a sense of alienation from God, neighbor, and self. We each meet death in our own way. The community of faith is there to support, pray, and guide if guidance is needed and wanted. But they are also there simply to be present, aiming to make sure no one dies alone.

The movie *Into the Woods* includes a song that makes the improbable claim "No one is alone. Truly. No one is alone."[19] Unfortunately, there are people who die alone. They have either outlived all their friends and relatives ("orphaned adults" as one person has said), or they have become alienated from all whom they once knew. For whatever reason, they find themselves facing death alone. There is a program called "No One Dies Alone," where volunteers provide a presence to dying patients who would otherwise have no one with them as they face death. In its original form, this program recruited volunteers from the hospital staff, including the support staff, to be with patients when they were dying. Christians can volunteer for similar programs—not with the intension of proselytizing but out of a commitment to Christian discipleship and to serving the least of the brothers and sisters in Christ.

When both patient and family readily acknowledge that death is imminent, one can affirm that a person's unique opportunity in life exists up until the time of death. Dying persons can make the most of the limited time the illness allows by doing the things they find most compelling, by making amends with people they have harmed, by seeking to forgive those who have harmed them, and by sharing memories and gratitude for the good things life has given them. None of that is possible if others require them to assume the role of the sick person fighting to be cured until their last breath.

Glorifying God as we face death will be impossible from the beginning if no one allows us—or if we ourselves refuse—to talk about death, to admit we are dying, to face the reality that no additional treatment will postpone death for long, and to be honest about how we feel, including what we fear. And, of course, the opposite is true as well. If someone prematurely or casually or cruelly insists that we accept our fate and let go of life too readily, the opportunity to glorify God as we face death will be diminished if not completely destroyed.

A final important aspect of vocation is the affirmation that God is free to call individuals into different tasks according to their own gifts and graces. In a broader context, this affirmation refuses to allow societal notions of gender or race to dictate what individuals are allowed and encouraged to pursue. But this final affirmation can also be made in the context of our expectations of what dying patients should do. Elisabeth Kübler-Ross's identification of the five stages of grief for terminal patients (denial, anger, bargaining, depression, and acceptance), which will be discussed further in chapter 5, has too often been interpreted not only as reactions many terminal patients experience but as stages that the best of them move through, one after another in progression until that final, blissful stage of acceptance is in hand.[20]

Sometimes ministers or chaplains believe it is their responsibility to make sure a patient's journey from anger to acceptance occurs. In reality it takes finesse and sensitivity and a gift for listening and discerning what's really being said when one listens to a person facing death. We are called to acknowledge the gifts and graces of the person facing a terminal illness and avoid imposing any sense that one needs to be led or manipulated through the stages of denial, anger, bargaining, and depression until one can finally claim acceptance. The last thing we want is for patients to be dishonest about how they feel. Withholding those feelings from some individual family members or friends may be an act of love, but someone should be present to encourage those who are dying to be honest about their fears, faltering faith, anger, or disappointments. Surely being given the opportunity to express how one feels honestly and deal with what is at stake in those feelings will more likely lead to a peaceful death than keeping those feelings a secret all the way to one's last breath in this world.

PRAYING FOR MIRACLES

A close look at Christian practices surrounding death—which are far more prevalent in the Roman Catholic tradition than for most Protestants—goes beyond the scope of this chapter. But a word about the practice of praying for a miracle will conclude the theological reflections set forth here. Prayer can reflect both the belief that death is the enemy to be fought against and the belief that death must be accepted as part of what it means to be mortal. Praying for a miracle, however, can get in the way of accepting and preparing for death.

Dayna Olson-Getty says that she and her husband were glad to be the recipient of whatever prayers others had to offer—including those who said, "I'm praying for a miracle"—when the baby she was carrying was diagnosed with a fatal birth defect. They, however, were not praying for a miracle. As she said, it would take "the ex nihilo, flesh-and-bone-creating kind of miracle for Ethan to be made whole."[21] She knew that she and her husband were the parents of a child who would live only a few minutes or hours, if he survived until birth at all. All their energy was focused on how to be the parents of a child who could not live for long:

> I am not capable of praying for healing while simultaneously preparing for Ethan's death. I have to choose one or the other—the two possibilities are simply too much for me to hold together. Eric and I only have this one opportunity, now, in these days of waiting, to parent Ethan well. We don't want to waste this precious opportunity by denying the reality that his life will be very short or by failing to acknowledge that what he needs most from us is our preparation to care for him in his dying.[22]

This does not, however, mean that Dayna Olson-Getty does not believe in miracles. She says that she has taken great comfort "in the miracle that is already assured—the miracle that Ethan's life will not end with his death, but will be joined to the eternal life of the God who made him." This comfort does not take away her grief, but she says that it means her son is just like all of us: "Our bodies are frail and fallible too, and they will all die sooner or later, but we have the promise of resurrection into a life that is not constrained by our frailty and that comes from the One who breathed life into all creation."[23]

An instrumental view of prayer is often found at the bedside

of those who are dying: If we just pray hard enough, some
people say, perhaps the terminal illness will be reversed. But
prayer is not to be understood as filling in the gap for what
medicine cannot do. Prayer and faith are not forms of magic
against death, and very little comfort is found in hearing that if
your faith were stronger, if you just prayed harder, you would
be healed. In making faithful decisions at the end of life, even
in prayer, there comes a time to accept that death is imminent
and no miraculous healing is at hand. But in prayer we are
reminded with Dayna Olson-Getty and with W. H. Auden
that the miracle has already happened:

> And because of His visitation, we may no
> Longer desire God as if He were lacking: our
> Redemption is no longer a question of pursuit
> But of surrender to Him who is always and
> Everywhere present. Therefore at every moment
> We pray that, following Him, we may depart from
> Our anxiety into His peace.[24]

QUESTIONS FOR REFLECTION

1. If we decide in each situation whether to continue treatment or accept that death is near (rather than applying an
   absolute mandate to preserve life), what has to be in place
   for us to stop treatment?
2. Do you agree that life can still have meaning and purpose
   even when an illness has severely diminished a patient's
   physical or mental abilities? Is there a point at which you
   believe life would no longer hold meaning for you?
3. Does the phrase "glorifying God" mean anything to you?
   Do you believe people can glorify God as they die? In what
   ways?
4. What does praying for a miracle mean to you? What do
   you believe is the relationship between prayer and medical
   treatment?

3

Assisted Death and Death-with-Dignity Laws

If U.S. society can't agree on withdrawal of life support, it is not surprising we also can't agree whether physicians should be able to prescribe a lethal dose of drugs to a terminally ill patient. The tension embedded in this debate is reflected in the language each side uses to make a case either for or against it. To understand the debate we need to examine the language.

Most people who support death-with-dignity laws use the term "physician-assisted death" rather than "physician-assisted suicide" (PAS), although originally the latter was the accepted phrase. Since death-with-dignity laws allow terminally ill patients to take a lethal dose of prescribed drugs to end their lives, avoiding the word *suicide* strikes some people as misleading. The word *suicide* is rejected, however, because people with a terminal illness, unlike people who take their lives out of despair or because of mental illness, *want to live*. Living, however, is no longer an option: they know they are going to die. Death-with-dignity laws provide them one of the few avenues they have left for controlling the situation: to choose when and how they will die instead of allowing the disease to make that choice for them, all the while robbing them of the pleasures of daily life. Brittany Maynard, who at twenty-nine was diagnosed with terminal brain cancer, insisted that she was not suicidal when she decided to end her life before the tumor did. "I've had the medication for weeks," she wrote. "I am not suicidal. If I were, I would have consumed that medication long ago. I do not want to die. But I am dying. And I want to die on my own terms."[1]

Supporters of death-with-dignity laws also tend to avoid the term *euthanasia* because of its association with eugenics programs, which employed involuntary euthanasia in an attempt to rid society of "undesirables," but also because technically it refers to a physician directly administering a lethal substance or injection, acts that remain illegal in the United States. "Aid in dying" is another phrase supporters employ rather than "suicide," and "medical aid in dying" (MAID) is the phrase commonly used in Canada. And, of course, the phrase used to describe state laws that legalize aid in dying, "death with dignity," reflects a positive attitude regarding what the legalization of physician-assisted death can accomplish: dignity at the time of death.

Opponents of these laws reject the phrase "physician assistance in dying," saying that it blurs the moral distinction between giving appropriate assistance—whether medical, emotional, or spiritual—to a person who is dying and acting in such a way that brings about death. Opponents readily employ the phrase "assisted suicide," insisting there is no moral distinction between physician-assisted death and suicide in general. Opponents also readily use the term *euthanasia*, preferring its negative connotations. Furthermore, the phrase "death-with-dignity law" does not represent their understanding of what is at stake in legalizing physician-assisted death. For them, dignity in death and dying cannot be found in taking one's life.

These disagreements over language are not petty arguments over semantics. They represent deep-seated disagreements in philosophical or theological beliefs about the ethics of resisting and accepting death. The language used can also affect the position people embrace. When surveys frame the issue by asking whether a physician should be allowed "to end the patient's life by some painless means," rather than in terms of euthanasia or assisting in suicide, approval of the action increases by nearly 20 percent.[2] Because I support the adoption of death-with-dignity laws, the term used in this chapter will be "physician-assisted death," unless quoting or referring to someone else's argument. Readers, however, should consider which term they believe is most appropriate: "physician-assisted death," "medical aid in dying," "physician-assisted suicide," "euthanasia," or some other term.

The first "euthanasia bill" was introduced in the United States in Ohio in 1906 (it didn't pass), and the Euthanasia Society of America was founded in New York in 1938, changing its name to the Society for the Right to Die in 1974. The history of debate over assisted death is complex and worthy of attention. For our purposes, however, it is sufficient to note that public debate in the United States was reignited in the 1990s when the citizens of Oregon were deciding whether to adopt a death-with-dignity law (which they did in 1998), and Jack Kevorkian was engaged in his highly publicized efforts to help people die—not all of whom were terminally ill.

The public debate continued as other states considered death-with-dignity laws and escalated again in 2014 when twenty-nine-year-old Brittany Maynard, mentioned above, made public her decision to end her life after being diagnosed with brain cancer and even after neurosurgery was given less than a year to live, with or without further treatment. Had the brain cancer taken its course, she could have experienced changes in personality and diminished cognitive and motor skills; also, terminal sedation could eventually have been required to control her pain. Not wanting to experience any of those things, she and her husband moved from California, where assisted death was then illegal, to Oregon in time to establish residency and take advantage of Oregon's death-with-dignity law. She became an outspoken public advocate of death-with-dignity laws before ending her life on November 1, 2014, having left a now well-known farewell on her Facebook page:

Goodbye to all my dear friends and family that I love. Today is the day I have chosen to pass away with dignity in the face of my terminal illness, this terrible brain cancer that has taken so much from me but would have taken so much more. The world is a beautiful place, travel has been my greatest teacher, my close friends and folks are the greatest givers. I even have a ring of support around my bed as I type. Goodbye world. Spread good energy. . . . Pay it forward.[3]

Her decision and her advocacy were reported in major newspapers and debated online, generating both fierce support and equally aggressive opposition to her decision.

Although the U.S. Supreme Court ruled in two cases in 1997 (*Vacco v. Quill* and *Washington v. Glucksberg*) that there is no constitutionally protected right to die, it did not declare death-with-dignity laws unconstitutional. Hence, the decision is left to each state. States can legalize physician-assisted death in one of three ways, which seven states and the District of Columbia have done at the time of this writing: by popular vote (Oregon, 1997, and Washington State, 2009); by an act of the state legislature (Vermont, 2013; California, 2016;[4] Colorado, 2016; and Hawaii, 2018); or by simply decriminalizing physician-assisted death without enacting a specific law (Montana, 1998). Washington DC's death-with-dignity law went into effect in January 2017. Outside those seven states and the District of Columbia, helping someone to take his or her life— even a terminally ill person—is considered assisting in a crime and is a felony.

There are, of course, restrictions embedded in death-with-dignity laws. Physicians write the prescription for a lethal dose of drugs but are not allowed to administer the drugs directly. No one is. While others can dissolve the drugs in a drink, the patient must be able to hold the glass and drink without assistance. Administering the lethal drugs directly is considered euthanasia, which is against the law in all fifty states. In this way, U.S. laws stand in contrast to the law adopted by Canada in June 2016, which allows physicians and nurse practitioners to administer a lethal dose of drugs directly (including by injection), although patients may choose to ingest the drugs unaided. In the United States, some physicians who prescribe the drugs choose to be present at the time the patient takes the lethal dose, but they are not required to be there. The patient who receives such a prescription must have a prognosis (confirmed by two doctors) of six months or less to live and make a request in writing. The patient has to be competent, and doctors have the right to require a psychological evaluation. Each patient must be informed of other options, including palliative and hospice care, and patients may change their minds at any time prior to taking the drugs. In fact, about a third of the patients who fill the prescription take it home and never use it.

Each side of the debate evaluates these safeguards embedded in the law differently. According to the organization Death with Dignity, these safeguards keep the laws from posing any danger at all, pointing to studies of Oregon's and Washington's death-with-dignity laws that show no evidence of coercion or abuse. The Heritage Foundation disagrees, claiming that the "purported safeguards in PAS [physician-assisted suicide] are ripe for abuse."[5] The adequacy of safeguards as evaluated by both sides will be addressed further as this chapter examines arguments for and against death-with-dignity laws.

Representatives from three groups of people in the United States have provided the most vocal opposition to assisted death: Christians, disability-rights organizations, and physicians. There are, however, other Christians, people with disabilities, and physicians who *support* the legalization of physician-assisted death, often in greater numbers than their opponents. In what follows, arguments against assisted death by representatives of these three groups will be described, and arguments in favor of assisted death by representatives of these same three groups will be offered in response. Although my agreement with death-with-dignity laws will be clear, the goal is to give a fair hearing to both sides. I may at times seek to be persuasive, but I do not believe an argument can be persuasive if it does not take into careful account the opposing point of view, giving credit to points well made while avoiding caricature and sarcasm, which too often make their way into this debate.

CHRISTIAN PERSPECTIVES

At least three theological affirmations inform the position of Christians who oppose assisted death: (1) divine sovereignty, which affirms that God alone gives life and can take life away; (2) the relational nature of Christian faith, which challenges an emphasis on individual autonomy; and (3) the sanctification of suffering. Christians who support assisted death can also affirm divine sovereignty and challenge an exclusive emphasis on individual autonomy. They will not, however, give as positive a role to human suffering or express the expectation that we must endure whatever suffering comes our way as Christians who oppose death-with-dignity laws may do.

Divine Sovereignty. Christians who are against physician-assisted death often rely on divine sovereignty, claiming that because our lives belong to God alone, we should not thwart God's purposes by ending life even in a situation of impending death. Christian ethicist Allen Verhey lifts up as exemplary terminally ill Christians who find both comfort and courage in knowing their lives belong not to them but to God. Their courage and comfort, he says, lead them to forego both medicalized dying *and* assisted suicide, insisting that there is a significant moral difference between "suicide and letting go our desperate hold on life."[6] Christians must not take their own lives even when death for them is near and, presumably, even when the indignities and pain that accompany death are acute. Christians need instead to put all their efforts into tending to the needs of dying persons through pain management, being present, and making them comfortable—not helping them take their own lives.

It is very common for Christians who refer to divine sovereignty in their opposition to physician-assisted death to claim that such an act is tantamount to "playing God." Such is the case with the conservative evangelical Eric Metaxas in an essay titled "Assisted Suicide—Like Playing God—Is Always Wrong."[7] Metaxas expresses astonishment that one Christian research team found that 38 percent of white evangelical Protestants agree with the following statement: "When a person is facing a painful terminal disease, it is morally acceptable to ask for a physician's aid in taking his or her own life."[8] This finding signals the surprising fact that many Christians who take a conservative stance on other moral and social issues support physician-assisted death. Metaxas, however, insists that it is not a viable Christian stance. Because God gives life, and God takes it away, both abortion and assisted death are murder. "Playing God," Metaxas insists, "is *always* wrong, whether at the beginning of life—*or* at its end."[9]

The idea that Christians who support physician-assisted death are rejecting the faithful affirmation that our lives are not our own is, I believe, misguided. Christians who support assisted death can readily respond to the first question of the Heidelberg Confession, mentioned in chapter 2, "What is your only comfort, in life and in death?" by reciting the response "That I am not my own, but belong—body and soul, in life and in death—to my faithful Savior, Jesus Christ."[10] Acknowledging that one's life is not one's own but belongs to God can *accompany* support for physician-assisted death.

First, anyone who has experienced a life-threatening illness that requires multiple doctors' visits and hospital stays knows that it is almost impossible to claim one's life as one's own. The disease redefines every aspect of life: the ability to sleep well, to walk with a steady gate or to walk at all, or to breathe in and out on one's own and without pain. When hospitalized, one's schedule of rising, sleeping, and eating will be taken over by members of the medical team, who must move to the rhythm of a medication schedule, the need to take vital signs, and overseeing treatments and tests. An almost singular focus on one's malfunctioning body can overshadow all other concerns as well as the joys of daily living.

Given that individuals with a life-threatening disease have often already lost control of their lives, efforts to take back what little control is left does not indicate a denial that God is sovereign or even an insistence that one avoid being dependent on others. Saying one wants to die on one's own terms does not set one against "God's terms" but challenges the terms set forth by the disease. It is possible for Christians to decide that they will not be reduced to either unbearable pain or terminal sedation before death and yet still entrust their lives—body and soul—to God as they face what the disease—*not God*—will soon do to them. Accepting the inevitability of death and hastening what is already about to happen does not represent an excessive claim to one's life but a way to accept one's death while remaining the recognizable self whom God has created and called us to be.

Second, the charge of "playing God" should be rejected because it is vague and used in contradictory ways. As noted in chapter 3, when doctors wanted to withdraw a respirator from Helga Wanglie, who was in a permanent vegetative state, her husband refused, insisting that we cannot play God. Nancy Cruzan's father insisted that if others thought he was playing God by requesting that his daughter's feeding tube be removed, he was willing to live with that charge.[11] In a highly publicized case in 1973, Dax Cowart said that doctors were playing God by forcing him to endure extremely painful, albeit life-saving treatments for burns even when he pleaded with them to stop.[12]

One can ask whether medicine is assuming the role of "playing God" by *not* letting someone die and by making every effort to keep a person alive, even when medical intervention does nothing but extend dying. One can also ask whether someone is assuming god-like control by insisting that a terminally ill patient face all the suffering, limitations, pain, and indignities that the disease hands out when medical intervention can no longer control them. The phrase "playing God" should be set aside altogether, and instead Christians should consider how to serve God's purposes for the specific suffering human being who stands before us. For some terminal patients, palliative care will allow them to see their way to the end, and some will accept the option of terminal sedation. But others will find that no amount of medication will control the pain, that terminal sedation seems pointless, and that all the indignities the illness will meet out make life not worth living. It is understandable that physician-assisted death is a line some Christians cannot cross, but it is disturbing when these same Christians claim that no person of true faith can take the lethal cocktail that hastens death.

Autonomy. Unlike those years in which doctors alone were given the authority to make medical decisions on behalf of a patient, including when to withdraw treatment, patients now have the right to make decisions about their own end-of-life care. Virtually no one argues for returning to the days when patients had no say in whether to accept, deny, continue, or withdraw treatment, although some rightly bemoan the consumerist turn patient autonomy has taken. Some Christians, however, challenge the notion of individual autonomy, even without the consumerist twist, as contradicting the relational character of the Christian life. "Relationships are not just part of our flourishing," Allen Verhey insists. "They are intrinsic to our identity as persons. We are born and live and die as persons-in-relation."[13] Christians should reject society's tendency to emphasize individual autonomy, especially when it leads to the idea that terminally ill patients can choose to end their lives when their illness becomes overly burdensome. Christians are called to avoid making independent and autonomous decisions and instead are called to rely on the assistance of people around us as we face the pain and debilitating effects that come with terminal illness.

Christians who support assisted death can agree that unqualified autonomy is not, in fact, a Christian value. Christians understand themselves as individuals *who are part of the body of Christ.* What we do, including the decisions we make at the end of life, are not about us alone: "The eye cannot say to the hand, 'I have no need of you,' nor again the head to the feet, 'I have no need of you'" (1 Cor. 12:21–22). Choosing assisted death, however, does not preclude conversations with other people or considerations of how such an act will affect others, or, in fact, the need to depend on others for support prior to the moment of taking the lethal dose of drugs when the chosen time has arrived.

Although not speaking from a Christian perspective, Derek Humphry, in his book *Final Exit*, which instructs terminally ill people on how to take their own lives, encourages people with terminal illness to talk to their family and friends before making such a serious decision.[14] Patient autonomy guarantees that patients have the primary say in treatment at the end of life—a right that should never be forfeited. Patients, however, do not have to emphasize their individual autonomy when making moral decisions in relation to the doctor, family, or other members of the Christian community to which they belong.

In questioning the value of patient autonomy, some Christians (as well as medical staff and ethicists) are rightly concerned when they hear that one of the motivations terminally ill patients have stated for their wish to die is not wanting to be a burden on others. Their concern arises over the possibility that family members have grown weary of the demands of time, stress, and money required to care for a terminally ill family member and may seek to persuade a patient to believe that death would be a blessing for the family. Might family members encourage or manipulate the patient to go the route of assisted death to ease the emotional and financial burden on the family or to ensure a larger inheritance, all the while seeming to support the patient's right to an autonomous decision? One can understand why a patient's concern over being a burden presents a red flag for the medical team and for ethicists.

This potential abuse, however, should not allow us to ignore the fact that some patients reach a point where no matter how much family members are willing to continue offering care, they become weary with their increasing dependency on others for the fundamental requirements of daily living. Even if we acknowledge that Christians should allow their autonomy to erode while they depend on others, some people have a clear limit regarding how much dependence they can tolerate. Also, and perhaps most important, the Christian faith does not give some people the authority to make unsolicited decisions for others. Brittany Maynard wanted the choice she made to be available to everyone who wanted it, but she resisted telling others what course to take, and she insisted that others could not dictate what she was required to endure:

> I would not tell anyone else that he or she should choose death with dignity. My question is: Who has the right to tell me that I don't deserve this choice? That I deserve to suffer for weeks or months in tremendous amounts of physical and emotional pain? Why should anyone have the right to make that choice for me?[15]

While absolute autonomy is inconsistent with Christian faith, allowing people the freedom to make decisions about when and where to die if dying is indeed already imminent is not.

The Sanctification of Suffering. Christians who oppose assisted death often argue that while the suffering that can accompany terminal illness should be alleviated to the extent possible by medical intervention, pain also needs to be endured in faith. When Brittany Maynard made public her plans to take her life, Kara Tippetts, a thirty-six-year-old evangelical Christian and mother of four young children who had been diagnosed with terminal breast cancer, wrote an open letter to Brittany Maynard. In her message, she spoke of Christian faith, suffering, and death:

> Brittany, . . . You have been told a lie. A horrible lie, that your dying will not be beautiful. That the suffering will be too great. . . . Yes, your dying will be hard, but it will not be without beauty. Hastening death was never what God intended. But in our dying, He does meet us with His beautiful grace.[16]

Conservative evangelical Christians like Kara Tippetts do not intend to glorify suffering but to sanctify it, believing that God may have a purpose in our suffering. They thus believe that alleviating suffering by directly choosing death is out of bounds in Christian faith.

Christians who favor physician-assisted death can, however, question Kara Tippetts's claim that God's grace does not meet someone when death is hastened by drugs as well as her claim that suffering is beautiful. Jessica Kelley, another evangelical Christian, posted a response to Kara Tippetts's letter, insisting that suffering at the end of life is not always beautiful. Having lost her young son to brain cancer she wrote,

> Trust me, *Brittany has been told the truth.* My son's death was not beautiful. His suffering was great. . . . At first we were able to manage his pain with modern medication, but as the tumor grew, the pain would find a way to exceed the medication's capabilities. He would often wake with a scream, gripping his head as the pressure increased from the fluids trapped within his skull.[17]

She concluded, "There is no place in the Bible that says death is beautiful. It stands among the powers and principalities and is the last enemy to be defeated by Christ."[18]

Christians are a diverse group in terms of theological affirmations and how those affirmations inform their stance on physician-assisted death. The disagreement over the legalization of death-with-dignity laws has no compromise; either one is in favor of its legalization or one is opposed, and no theological argument on one side or the other will finally bring about consensus. We can, however, listen respectfully to the best points offered by each side and refuse to caricature or belittle those with whom we disagree, and we should, I believe, refrain from claiming that no faithful Christian can take advantage of a death-with-dignity law even if we strongly disagree with such an action.

DISABILITY RIGHTS

One group within the disability rights community, Not Dead Yet, has been especially outspoken, one could say strident, in its opposition to physician-assisted death. The organization spoke out against Jack Kevorkian's reckless actions in the 1990s and against every state campaign to adopt death-with-dignity laws. Not Dead Yet, which its founder named after a Monty Python song, calls itself on its website "The Resistance" and describes the organization as "a national, grassroots disability rights group that opposes legalization of assisted suicide and euthanasia as deadly forms of discrimination."[19] The organization not only believes existing safeguards are inadequate to protect people with disabilities but also claims that no safeguards can protect people with disabilities from abuse and even wrongful death.

The Slippery Slope. The primary argument against assisted death set forth by Not Dead Yet and other disability rights advocates is based on the logic of the slippery slope: If we allow individuals with a terminal illness access to physician-assisted death, people with disabilities and the elderly will be pressured to take their own lives and eventually even have their lives taken from them against their will in acts of involuntary euthanasia. Supporters of assisted death often readily dismiss the slippery slope as a philosophical fallacy, but to ensure moral integrity we cannot, in fact, ignore it. Intellectual honesty requires us to consider whether it is *possible* for the position we hold to carry us to a more extreme stance than we intend. Some vulnerable members of society, such as elderly patients in nursing facilities, are already abused, and their care can be burdensome and costly, so we must invoke the slippery slope and ask whether someone would try to coerce them into choosing death or even directly administer a lethal dose of drugs against their will if death-with-dignity laws were enacted.

The fallacy of the slippery slope, however, occurs when one assumes the slide into a more radical action than one originally intends is inevitable. Just because abuse *can* occur does not mean it *will* occur. States with death-with-dignity laws have put safeguards in place to thwart the slide into dangerous actions. Oregon's law, for instance, states that no person qualifies for physician assistance in dying "solely because of age or disability." In other words, having a disability does not in itself make one eligible to take advantage of the law. One must have a terminal illness and a prognosis of six months or less to live.

But that response alone is not sufficient to address the concerns of disability rights advocates who invoke the slippery slope. Death-with-dignity laws, they say, gain momentum from and then increase negative attitudes about people with disabilities. People with severe disabilities are already made to feel that their lives are not worth living. When someone says that disabilities resulting from a terminal illness make life no longer worth living, it can increase society's devaluation of people who are already disabled. Gloria Maxson, for instance, objected to the underlying premise of the film *Whose Life Is It Anyway?* for its sympathetic portrayal of the protagonist fighting for the right to die after being paralyzed in a car accident. Maxson says that the film suggests "the life of a disabled person could not be worth living, and should thus be 'mercifully' terminated by suicide or euthanasia."[20] As someone with polio and arthritis, and hence one who uses a wheelchair, she strongly protests that message, saying that her life, along with the lives of her friends with disabilities, "has genuine value in the sight of God—and humanity." The film, she says, reflects the attitude of many people whom she encounters who say, "If I were you, I'd kill myself." As she points out, "it's just a small step from that to, 'And why *don't* you?'"[21]

Gloria Maxson's perspective should be heeded. Believing that life with a disability is not a life worth living may have a profound effect on the person who has been recently disabled because of a life-threatening disease and who cannot imagine living with the various disabilities that may accompany it. Individuals who have learned that they will never be able to do things that once defined the life they knew need time to adjust and certainly should not make life-and-death decisions if still reeling from the news or depressed about the staggering change in life circumstances.

Many people, who from accident or illness can no longer do the things they once could, find that over time they can adjust to things they once thought would be intolerable. Great caution needs to be used in addressing a terminally ill person's request for assisted death, making sure the decision is not the result of depression and giving the person time to adjust to becoming dependent on a wheelchair or otherwise being unable to do things once taken for granted. Nevertheless, we also have to recognize that some people who are dying reach a point where life has ceased to have value *for them*—no matter what others think. For some people, losing the capacity to work in the garden, or interact with children or grandchildren, or enjoy a meal, will make life lose its value. One woman's family, who was deciding whether to continue treatment that would leave her almost completely incapacitated, knew that among all the things their mother and wife would no longer be able to do, not being able to cook for people would tip the scales toward making life unbearable.[22] If that sounds shallow to some people, perhaps they are refusing to take this woman's life's story into account and are attempting to impose their values on her.

Even as we listen to the objections of disabilities rights organizations, we need to consider that some disability rights advocates *support* the legalization of physician-assisted death. When Canada was considering whether to adopt a medical-aid-in-dying law (which it did in June 2016), Canada's largest disability rights group (the Coalition of Provincial Organizations of the Handicapped, or COPOH), argued in favor of making assisted death available to people with disabilities who are terminally ill and who have decision-making capacities:

> COPOH argued that disabled persons have been historically victimized by stereotypical attitudes about their abilities and worth, coupled with a paternalism that has undercut their right to self-determination. Denying [terminally ill] people

with disabilities the option of suicide is an example of this unequal treatment, and must be resisted as demeaning and discriminatory.[23]

COPOH recognizes that people with disabilities may be in danger of believing that "their lives are worthless and burdensome and, as a result, contemplate suicide." This danger, however, should not indicate that physician-assisted death in light of terminal illness be withheld from people with disabilities but that clear safeguards be put in place to ensure that vulnerable populations are protected from abuse even as their autonomy is not diminished.[24]

Some people with disabilities are, in fact, angry because they cannot take advantage of physician-assisted death even when it is legal. People in the last stages of ALS (amyotrophic lateral sclerosis), for instance, cannot take the lethal dose of drugs unassisted, which by law they must be able to do, and may not even be able to swallow. Typically they are not within six months of dying when they are still capable of taking the drugs. Being unable to take advantage of physician-assisted death, some people choose other forms of ending their lives before the disease runs its course. VSED ("voluntarily stopping eating and drinking") is one of those ways.

VSED refers to a decision made by a competent person suffering from an advanced illness who chooses to refrain from eating and drinking for the purpose of hastening death.[25] It does not refer to what happens when a dying person has no interest in eating or drinking, to someone who is no longer able to eat or drink, or to withdrawing food and drink from a patient involuntarily. VSED indicates a conscious decision made by competent patients to end their lives by refusing to eat or drink, and it is legal in all fifty states. Depending on their physical health, people who choose to stop eating and drinking typically live for seven to fourteen days. VSED can provide a peaceful way to die, especially for someone who is already frail, since hunger and thirst tend to subside after the first day or two, and some people even experience moments of euphoria.

It can, however, be extremely unpleasant, resulting in delirium and anxiety.

One dilemma presented by VSED arises when patients diagnosed with some form of dementia want to take their lives before losing all sense of self. No death-with-dignity law will allow them access to physician-assisted death unless they have a prognosis of six months or less to live, and by the time such a prognosis is made, they will no longer be competent. If someone who has voluntarily stopped eating and drinking begins to ask for food and water, it *must* be provided no matter what instructions the patient may have previously given. Patient autonomy demands that a person's immediate wishes be followed—not the wishes that were expressed earlier if the patient contradicts them now. If someone wants to begin eating and drinking again, food and water must be given.[26]

It is critical that Christians who support death-with-dignity laws be unwavering in the affirmation that Christian faith does not allow us to say that any person's life has ceased to have value or has become useless when facing the limitations imposed by disabilities, whether the result of terminal illness or not. No matter what the situation, no matter how bad the pain or distorted the body, a dying person's life does *matter*. Disability rights organizations, however, are not protecting all disabled people from discrimination, nor do they speak for all disabled persons when they oppose death-with-dignity laws.

PHYSICIANS

In 2014 a survey conducted by Medscape found that over half (54 percent) of the 21,000 physicians surveyed indicated support for physician-assisted death, marking the first time a majority of physicians expressed this point of view.[27] This does not, however, mean that the controversy in the medical community is over or even that physicians who support death-with-dignity laws are prepared to comply with a terminally ill patient's request for the lethal dose of drugs. Although many aspects of the Hippocratic oath are ignored today, the well-known imperative from the oath has long influenced physicians to stand against medical aid in dying: "I will neither give a fatal drug to anyone if I am asked for it, nor will I make a suggestion to this effect."[28] Any number of factors are at stake as physicians consider death-with-dignity laws: the well-entrenched mind-set that medicine is for cure and care, not killing; fear of losing a patient's trust if they assist someone in dying; fear of the slippery slope; the doctrine of double effect; and the belief that there are alternatives to assisted death, such as hospice and palliative care.

Cure, Not Killing. As emphasized in chapter 1, physicians are trained to focus their efforts almost exclusively on *cure*—even when cure is no longer possible. Admitting that the next round of treatment will do no good and turning their efforts to care can present a challenge. Taking the additional and serious step of prescribing a lethal dose of drugs that patients will use to end their lives is unthinkable for many physicians. For some physicians, a deep-seated understanding of the value of human life based on religious or philosophical values accompanies their emphasis on cure and care, making the direct taking of life a morally reprehensible act.

The commitment to cure and care is so well ingrained that even doctors who support death-with-dignity laws may find it difficult to comply with a terminally ill patient's request for the lethal dose of drugs. Jessica Zitter, who supports a patient's right to make that request, says that she equivocated the first time a patient asked her for assistance in dying. While she was right to persuade him to allow a little more time while she treated his depression, she admits that she was not comfortable with the idea of helping any patient die—nor was she prepared. She believes physicians who are willing to write the prescription need "formal protocols, official procedures, outcome measurements, even a certificate of expertise issued by an oversight board."[29] Since all other medical procedures require training, she wonders why none of these things exist in any state where physician-assisted death is legal.

Trust. Along with being committed to curing their patients, physicians fear that they will lose the trust of patients who know they are willing not only to relinquish attempts at cure but also to help their patients die. Won't their patients feel abandoned if they end all medical care and write a prescription aimed at the patient's death? In the documentary *How to Die in Oregon,* a patient receives notice from his insurance company that while insurance will not pay for the next round of treatments, which doctors had determined would do him no good, it would cover the cost of drugs if he sought to take advantage of physician-assisted death.[30] The man was understandably angry and did, indeed, feel abandoned.

On the other hand, patients can lose trust in their physicians when physicians are unwilling to prescribe the lethal dose of drugs and abandon them to symptoms that cannot be relieved with medical intervention. Elizabeth Willner, for instance, who was a resident of California with stage-4 colon cancer that had metastasized to the liver and lungs, was turned down by three physicians when she requested the drugs to end her life. "'I understand that bumping off your patients isn't why you went to medical school,' she said. 'But I believe it falls squarely within the Hippocratic oath because making me drown in bodily fluids is doing more harm than giving me the prescription.'"[31] Trust works both ways. Physicians need to ensure patients that they will not be abandoned when the disease does its worst, but some patients want to trust their physicians to help them die when the disease becomes unbearable and will, in fact, feel abandoned if they won't.

Trust demands a relationship between physician and patient. This is one of the problems with Jack Kevorkian's approach to helping people die. Kevorkian was known for helping patients die only a day or two after meeting them and without getting to know them and with no second opinion to confirm his decision. Establishing trust with a patient, especially when embarking on such a serious action, can happen in a relatively short time, but it demands paying attention to the patient's story, determining whether the patient is depressed, and asking whether alternatives have been offered and considered. The physician Timothy Quill is well known as a doctor who prescribed medication that he knew his long-time patient would take to end her life. In 1991 he published an essay in the *New England Journal of Medicine* that describes how and why he prescribed barbiturates to a forty-five-year-old woman with a severe form of leukemia who didn't want to continue treatment. She had been his patient for many years, and he disagreed with her decision. But after extensive conversations with her and her family, he knew that she was "mentally alert and making her decision calmly, fully aware of all the alternatives."[32] His decision to help her was based on trust that had been established over a long period of time. What is tragic about the story is that neither he nor Diane's family could be with her when she took the drugs for fear that they would be held legally responsible for her death. After saying goodbye to her husband and son, she died alone.

The Slippery Slope for Doctors. The slippery slope, as described above, comes into play when physicians consider their role in helping terminally ill patients die. If doctors are allowed to prescribe a lethal dose of drugs to terminally ill patients, what will prevent them from taking an additional step and making a decision on behalf of a patient and directly administering the drugs that kill? An anonymous essay titled "It's Over, Debbie," which appeared in the *Journal of the American Medical Association* in 1988, confirmed for some physicians the possibility of this fear being realized.[33] According to his own account, a resident was called in the middle of the night to see a twenty-year-old woman with terminal ovarian cancer and labored breathing. The only words the woman said were "Let's get this over," which the resident interpreted to mean the patient wanted to die. With little reflection and never having met the patient prior to this encounter, the resident decided to end the woman's pain—and life—by giving her an overdose of morphine. Many physicians expressed concern—if not horror—at this account. As Timothy Rowe put it in his 2014 essay titled "It's Still Not Over, Debbie," "During residency we become familiar with the idea that patients die, but this familiarity should not mean that hastening death becomes just another management option."[34]

The resident was never prosecuted because his or her identity was never uncovered, and the date and place of the physician's actions remain unknown. Some people even suspect the case was fictitious, intended only to promote discussion. There was indeed fierce debate over *JAMA*'s decision to publish what some, including the mayor of New York, Ed Koch, thought was a confession of murder. The essay is often cited now as a cautionary tale regarding what can happen even when physician aid in dying is *illegal*; once society decides that assisting someone in death is both moral and legal, what will prevent such actions from taking place again and even routinely? Interestingly, however, some physicians and many patients, especially those with terminal illness, and family members of patients who had died after long and unsuccessful treatments reacted positively to what the anonymous writer described, affirming the resident's compassion in responding to the patient's desire to be released from the now-unbearable effects of her disease. While invoking the slippery slope helps bring clarity to the argument, it does not identify what is right for everyone. Indeed, nothing can.

Slow Codes and Terminal Sedation. The situation is made more complex by the fact that physicians have for a very long time taken actions that hasten a patient's death. These actions include a slow code and terminal sedation. A slow code may occur when a medical team knows that CPR will not revive a patient and will, in fact, do more harm than good but a DNAR order is not in place. Rather than the rapid, almost frantic, movement of a team responding to a code, the movement toward resuscitation in a slow code is delayed so that perhaps the patient will die before being put through the violent, and in these cases ineffective, actions involved in CPR. Slow code is not an official code called over the intercom but a decision made by individual members of the medical team who know that resuscitation will cause additional suffering with no reasonable possibility of reviving the patient. If this sounds dangerously irresponsible, consider the danger to a patient's well-being when a code is performed on someone for whom it was never intended. Jessica Zitter describes such a situation:

> The patient's skin is an ashy gray-yellow with a waxy sheen. The abdomen is visible beneath the soiled sheets, deflated from years of malnourishment and disease. A resident is already doing chest compressions, kneeling on the bed to get better leverage. With each compression, there is a sickening click, which I don't recognize until I hear someone next to me whisper, "His whole chest is breaking."[35]

CPR was not meant for frail patients, whose ribs will almost certainly break under the force of compressions, but full code is the default form of action for any patient who has not been designated DNAR. Sometimes when the medical team knows that CPR can only harm the patient, the typically rapid response to a code called over the intercom is slower, while members of the response team hope that the patient will die before CPR kills him instead.

Terminal sedation, which Brittany Maynard insisted she wanted to avoid, occurs when morphine or another drug is used to ease unrelenting pain, and it results in unconsciousness intended to last until the patient dies and perhaps even hastens death. As Haider Warraich points out, while some physicians want to rebrand terminal sedation by calling it "palliative sedation," others believe that it is not that different from euthanasia since a member of the medical staff administers the drug directly. One palliative-care physician, who supports the practice, prefers to call it "slow euthanasia." Some physicians find that they are willing to use terminal sedation with a clear conscience because of the doctrine of double effect.

Doctrine of Double Effect. A long-standing concept in Roman Catholic moral theology, the doctrine of double effect is also used by some Protestants and in secular ethics as well. The doctrine recognizes as significant a difference between the intended and unintended results of one's action even if the latter can be foreseen. In terminal sedation, for instance, the intent is to ease pain and anxiety while the unintended, but known, second effect is that the medication can hasten and may even cause death. Some ethicists, myself included, believe that the doctrine of double effect is problematic because it's dishonest. Since one does actually know what the unintended effect could be, how much moral weight can be given to the fact that it is not intended? Nevertheless, there are those physicians who, knowing that they do not intend the patient's death, are relieved of the moral stress of taking actions that may hasten death. Some of these same doctors, however, are not willing to take the next step into knowingly prescribing a lethal dose of drugs, which if used by the patient will have only one intended purpose—death. Whereas some people find the distinction between withdrawing treatment, a slow code, and terminal sedation to be morally negligible when considering physician-assisted death, others see the distinctions as critical and draw the line at the latter.

Alternatives. One of the most common and very significant objections to physician-assisted death is that there are alternatives. Hospice organizations have traditionally—albeit not always—been opposed to physician-assisted death and have insisted that many concerns expressed by dying patients can be addressed by hospice and specialists in palliative care. One of the benefits of the debate over assisted death is that more people have become aware of hospice and palliative care and taken advantage of their services. These branches of medical care, however, cannot always address a person's pain or other discomfort. Jessica Kelley, whose child was dying said, "The pain would find a way to exceed the medication's capabilities."[36] The documentary *How to Die in Oregon* describes a man whose brain tumor began to press upon his eyes until he couldn't close his eyelids. No medical intervention could address his pain.

And pain isn't actually the primary reason people have taken advantage of death-with-dignity laws: loss of autonomy, decreasing ability to participate in activities that made life enjoyable, and loss of dignity are often cited as the primary reasons people want to take advantage of a death-with-dignity law. It may sound like doublespeak to say that protecting life leads us to support assisted death, but I believe it does. We are protecting the integrity of life for people with debilitating, life-threatening, and sometimes acutely painful conditions by giving them control over when and how they die so that they can face death on their own terms and not let death control the final weeks and hours of life.

QUESTIONS FOR REFLECTION

1. Do you agree that death-with-dignity laws should be legal? What arguments do you put forth to support or oppose these laws?
2. Do you believe that a faithful Christian can choose to take advantage of physician-assisted death?
3. Do people with disabilities have reason to fear that the slippery slope will go into effect once death-with-dignity laws are passed and that they will be in danger of becoming victims of coercion or even of involuntary euthanasia? Conversely, should people with disabilities be given the freedom to decide for themselves whether to take advantage of assisted death if facing a terminal illness?
4. Can patients lose trust in their physicians if they believe their doctor could be involved in physician-assisted death? Can patients lose trust in their physicians if they believe their doctor would refuse to be involved in physician-assisted death?

4

Physician-Patient Relations and Advance Directives

Being prepared to resist death when resisting remains a reasonable goal and being willing to accept death when treatment is no longer likely to preserve life in a meaningful way require extended conversations before the need to make a decision arises. We all need to talk to family members and appropriate friends as well as health-care providers about our end-of-life wishes and about the values that help define our lives. Most physicians, however, are notoriously unprepared to talk about death with their patients, although their reluctance is being challenged somewhat as palliative and hospice care are becoming more common, advance directives and POLST forms are more often in place, and some physicians are seeking reform. But we have a long way to go.

Furthermore, as we've seen in previous chapters, patients and their families are also unprepared to talk about death. They, too, need to be encouraged to face death more honestly and to talk about death before an urgent situation arises. Conversations about end-of-life care with family members and with one's physician can make a difference in what kind of care we receive. This chapter describes advance directives as well as POLST (physician orders for life-sustaining treatment) and gives brief attention to organ donation, which is included as an option on the advance-directive form. But before we look at advance directives, surrogate decision makers, and POLST

74

forms, an understanding of physician-patient relationships may help us approach our physicians with our end-of-life concerns.

PHYSICIAN-PATIENT RELATIONSHIPS

The theologian Paul Lehmann and the physician Atul Gawande, without ever being aware of each other's work, provide similar descriptions of three ways the physician-patient relationship can be described: (1) hierarchical or paternalistic; (2) egalitarian, or what Gawande calls the "informative" approach; and (3) what Paul Lehmann calls a pattern of reciprocal responsibility, identified by Gawande as the "interpretative" relationship.

Hierarchical and Paternalistic Pattern. In a hierarchical relationship, power flows—more or less exclusively—from the person in authority to the subordinate, in this case from physician to patient. The physician assumes (and is occasionally readily given) far more power in decision making than the patient and, sometimes, exclusive power. Gawande calls this paternalistic pattern the oldest and most traditional relationship between physician and patient and one that is still commonly found today. The physician's attitude is "We have the knowledge and experience. We make the critical choices. . . . We tell you only what we believe you need to know." It is, Gawande says, the "doctor-knows-best model."[1] We saw this pattern at work in the cases of Karen Ann Quinlan and Nancy Cruzan, and it still exists all these decades later.

Hierarchical relationships are often meant to be benevolent (hence, the fatherly image projected by the word *paternalism*), but they can be hostile. Many of us have encountered arrogant physicians who have no interest in talking to us as human beings. The physician can be something akin to an automobile mechanic, the expert who knows how to fix body parts, while the patient, unfortunately, becomes the car. As the expert, the mechanic makes all the decisions. But hierarchical relationships can also be compassionate. At its best, doctors can assume a paternalistic attitude toward the patient with all good intentions and in recognition of the real human being who is not just a patient whose parts need to be mended but a person the physician cares for.

Even at its best, however, there is something problematic in paternalistic relationships, which by definition treat patients as children who cannot make informed decisions about their own medical care. Some people believe paternalism is always wrong unless (1) the patient is limited in capacity (such as someone who is mentally confused) and (2) the intervention will prevent excessive harm. Furthermore, both of these conditions must be in play at the same time before one can accept the paternalistic pattern of relationship. The wishes of a Jehovah's Witness, for instance, whose refusal of treatment will most certainly cause harm and perhaps even death, should be honored if the person has full capacity for decision making. Apart from these two qualifications existing simultaneously, paternalism is problematic. First, individuals may know what is best for them far better than their physicians, who may not share their values, and second, a paternalistic attitude toward a patient can be too easily abused as it ignores a patient's rights.

When Gawande's father was diagnosed with a rare and life-threatening tumor, the first doctor he and his parents visited became impatient with the questions his father, who was also a physician, asked about the surgery. After tolerating the first few questions, the doctor became exasperated when he realized there were more questions to follow:

> He had the air of the renowned professor he was—authoritative, self-certain, and busy with things to do.
>   Look, he said to my father, the tumor was dangerous. He, the neurosurgeon, had a lot of experience treating such tumors. Indeed, no one had more. The decision for my father was whether he wanted to do something about his tumor. If he did, the neurosurgeon was willing to help. If he didn't, that was his choice.[2]

Gawande's father chose not to work with this physician.

For all the potential abuses of the hierarchical relationship, Paul Lehmann identifies one aspect that can be appreciated. While he is addressing human relationships in general, his ideas can be applied specifically to describe how physicians relate to their patients. According to Lehmann, hierarchy rightly recognizes an imbalance of power that actually exists in some relationships – in this case between the patient and the physician.[3] Not only does the physician have far more knowledge about the disease and treatments than the patient, but the patient is made vulnerable simply by virtue of being sick. While acknowledging this imbalance of power does not justify the tendency of paternalism to accentuate it, a failure to acknowledge this imbalance may do harm to the patient.

Egalitarianism, or the Informative Pattern Approach. Atul Gawande describes the "informative" relationship between the physician and patient as one where the doctor's attitude is "We tell you the facts and figures. The rest is up to you . . . the doctor is the technical expert. The patient is the consumer."[4] Here the assumption is that the doctor and the patient are equals and their relationship can be negotiated on a contractual understanding. This egalitarian pattern goes hand in hand with the consumerist turn we saw in the emphasis on patient autonomy, where medicine becomes a commodity and patients become consumers. The strength of the egalitarian model is that patient autonomy cannot be so easily set aside as in paternalism.[5] An adult patient, who is already vulnerable, is not treated as a child and made to feel even more disempowered. But the weakness of a naive or ideological egalitarianism is that it does not recognize the real differences in power between the patient and the doctor.[6] Egalitarianism can result in a cruel expectation that patients be more independent than they are able or even want to be.

Gawande gives an example of another oncologist who gave so much information regarding treatment options for his father's cancer that neither he nor his parents—all three of whom were doctors—could understand.[7] The physician was offering data, and his father was expected to make a choice.

They were overwhelmed by the sheer volume of information being presented, and as Gawande points out, the conversation never turned to what his father cared about, "which was finding a path with the best chance of maintaining a life he'd find worthwhile."[8] This, too, was not the physician Gawande's father chose.

Reciprocal Responsibility, or the Interpretive Relationship. The third pattern of relationship is identified by Lehmann as one of "reciprocal responsibility" and by Gawande as "interpretative." A relationship of reciprocal responsibility—unlike egalitarianism—acknowledges that an imbalance of power exists between the doctor and the patient. Unlike a hierarchical relationship, however, this relationship does not accentuate this imbalance but seeks to lessen the effect of it. It also recognizes that each partner—physician and patient—has something to give and something to learn in an encounter between two human beings. According to Gawande, "the doctor's role is to help patients determine what they want," but not by overwhelming them with information. Interpretative doctors, he says, ask, "What is most important to you? What are your worries?"[9] Another way to identify this relationship is to call it "shared decision making."

The third doctor Gawande and his parents visited was concerned about his father's goals of care:

> He recognized that my father's questions came from fear. So he took the time to answer them, even the annoying ones. Along the way, he probed my father, too. He said that it sounded like he was more worried about what the operation might do to him than what the tumor would. My father said he was right.[10]

This third physician looked his father in the eye and because he was a tall man, he even sat so that he was eye level with his patient. He listened to what Gawande's father needed to say before turning the conversation back to the issue of his cancer and treatment. Getting to know Gawande's father by listening to him led the physician to advise against surgery for the time being because he thought it didn't address all of the goals he heard his patient express. This was the physician Gawande's father chose to work with because he trusted him. "[The doctor] had made the effort to understand what my father cared about most," writes Gawande, "and to my father that counted for a lot."[11]

The physician Margaret Mohrmann suggests that this pattern of relationship requires the physician to "pay attention," pointing to Arthur Miller's *Death of a Salesman* to accentuate this point. As her husband's life begins to deteriorate, Willie Loman's wife says to her sons, "He's a human being, and a terrible thing is happening to him. So attention must be paid. He's not to be allowed to fall into his grave like an old dog. Attention, attention must be finally paid to such a person."[12] Mohrmann believes that "the practice of the ministry of medicine is the practice of paying attention," which "means, more than anything, listening to the stories [patients] have to tell us."[13] This approach, of course, requires sensitive listening on the part of the physician, recognizing that patients aren't always sure of what they want and that their goals may change as the disease and the treatments progress. It also requires time—something many physicians do not seem to have.

While Paul Lehmann and Atul Gawande believe the third relational pattern to be the most desirable, not all patients will agree. Some patients want their physician to assume a paternalistic role and make decisions for them. And as we've seen in chapter 1, some patients want to claim their right to make autonomous decisions and demand a certain kind of care and thus choose to be treated like informed consumers. Other, perhaps most, patients want their physicians to listen to them and help them define their goals of care. Of course, patients cannot dictate what kind of attitude a physician will bring to the physician-patient relationship. Physicians who assume a paternalistic approach are not likely to change just because patients want them to, and physicians who expect patients to process a great deal of medical information and make decisions may not be able to shift gears just because they are asked to do so.

Patients and family members should, however, be aware that not every physician and patient are a good fit. A highly skilled physician will not be the best physician for everyone. Depending on the medical situation, changing doctors may not always be possible, but it often is.

Atul Gawande and his parents chose not to stay with the paternalistic or the informative doctor and found instead a physician who was interested in his father's goals of care. Sometimes patients hesitate to change doctors for fear of hurting their physician's feelings or simply because it takes a great deal of effort to start over with someone else. But trust between a patient and physician is extremely important; patients who have a choice of doctors should consider carefully whether trust is possible with the doctor they now have.

ADVANCE DIRECTIVES

In addition to being attentive to the physician-patient relationship and gaging how one can best talk to a physician, patients can influence their end-of-life care by filling out an advance directive, talking to the person designated as surrogate decision maker, and talking to family members and to physicians if at all possible about their wishes. An advance directive is a document used to indicate in writing a person's wishes regarding medical treatment when that person is no longer able to make those wishes known. Although there once was a distinction made between a living will, which provides this information, and an advance directive, which indicates a designated surrogate decision maker, most people use the terms "living will" and "advance directive" interchangeably. Although "advance directive" is probably the better term, "living will" tends to dominate popular use. I tend to use the terms interchangeably to designate the combined document that indicates a surrogate decision maker and gives written instructions regarding end-of-life care.

Living wills were first proposed by people who had seen

someone close to them experience a slow death at a time when it was almost impossible to say no to treatment ordered by the physician. The first living will was suggested in 1967 by Luis Kutner, a human rights lawyer from Chicago, whose close friend died after a long and painful illness. He wanted to ensure that dying people had the right to make decisions regarding their own end-of-life medical care. Walter F. Sackett, inspired by Kutner, introduced a bill in the Florida State legislature that would give patients the right to make decisions regarding life-sustaining treatment. The bill failed in 1968 and again in 1973. In the meantime, Barry Keene subsequently presented a bill that promoted the use of living wills in the California State legislature in 1974. He was motivated by the experience of his mother-in-law, who had not been allowed to refuse treatment for a terminal illness. His bill passed in 1976, making California the first state to sanction living wills.[14]

As I indicated in chapter 1, the movement toward state adoption of living wills was significantly advanced when Chief Justice Robert Hughes wrote the decision of the New Jersey Supreme Court regarding Karen Ann Quinlan in 1976, affirming the right of patients to refuse treatment even if that decision would lead to death. He also ruled that someone else could exercise that right on behalf of a patient if the patient is mentally unable to do so. The decision in the Nancy Cruzan case also furthered the legitimacy of living wills (which she, like Karen Ann Quinlan, did not have) and surrogate decision makers. Because of the public nature of the Terri Schiavo case, many people were encouraged to render their end-of-life wishes in writing, indicating in their instructions that even if the president of the United States disagrees, no life-sustaining treatment should continue for them under similar conditions.

In 1990 the Patient Self-Determination Act (PSDA) was passed, requiring all medical facilities that receive Medicare and Medicaid benefits (such as hospitals, skilled nursing homes, home health agencies, and hospices) to have policies that provide written information to adult patients on admission about their rights to make medical decisions and to have advance directives. If an institution does not comply, the government may withhold Medicare benefits. This is why, on admission to a hospital, someone will ask you, "Do you have a living will?"[15]

While the sponsor of the Patient Self-Determination Act, Senator John Danforth from Missouri, had hoped that requiring these institutions to ask whether a patient has a living will would encourage conversation between physicians and their patients about end-of-life care, it has not. It has simply become a box for personnel in admitting areas to check. Although some hospitals will send a social worker to talk to a patient who has been admitted without a living will, not all hospitals do this, and no immediate conversation ensues if the patient when being admitted responds, "No, I don't have one," and for good reason. The admitting area of a hospital is not the appropriate place to prepare one's advance directive.

Jessica Zitter highlights this problem in her description of nursing facilities that pride themselves on being able to report a high rate of patients who *have* completed an advance directive on admission to their facility. This is admirable, of course, but Zitter identifies a serious problem in that the advance directives that she and her team receive from nursing homes tend to be "cookie-cutter similar":

> Almost all of them indicate that the patient wants every attempt to prolong life to be pursued. Rarely is a treatment considered unacceptable, regardless of the patient's prognosis. . . . And, sadly, this makes sense. Discussing values and preferences in the event of debilitation is complex, time-consuming, and often harrowing. And since nursing homes are paid to care for patients as long as they remain alive, are their employees really the right people to oversee the completion of these forms?[16]

Avoiding this cookie-cutter approach requires time that cannot be provided during admission to a nursing facility or hospital. Allen Verhey suggests that instead of relying on admission to a hospital or nursing facility to talk about advance directives, the church could adopt the writing of living wills as a

Christian practice. People could write their living wills in the context of the community of faith where they can "talk and think and pray about mortality," recognizing the church "as a community of moral discourse and discernment."[17] One could, of course, make a similar suggestion for any religious community.

Even though by 1992—over a quarter of a century ago—all fifty states had adopted a legal version of an advance directive, progress toward ensuring the rights of patients to make their own decisions regarding medical treatment has been slow. Court cases that ruled in favor of a patient's right to refuse treatment have provided no guarantee that patients' wishes would subsequently be honored. As we saw in chapter 1, the 1914 decision in *Schoendorff v. New York Charity Hospital*, claiming that doing surgery against a patient's will was assault, did not change the culture that increasingly emphasized a doctor's authority to determine treatment on behalf of a patient and even against a patient's will. Instead, physicians' authority increased as advances were made in medicine's ability to address once-incurable diseases, shifting the focus of medicine so acutely to cure that cure was pursued even when it was no longer appropriate and even if it went against what a patient wanted. Many people are surprised to learn that even today putting one's wishes in writing in a living will doesn't guarantee that what one wants will be honored. Considering the various ways that an advance directive can fail and avoiding those pitfalls can make it more likely that your advance directive will help guide others in making decisions about your end-of-life care consistent with your wishes when you can no longer speak for yourself.

Surrogates. Although a living will is a legal document that should be filled out in accordance with state law, it should be considered first and primarily as a means of communication. Checking a series of boxes and filing your living will with your lawyer is not sufficient to ensure that your wishes will be known and honored. The most important part of the document is naming a person and an alternate to make decisions on your behalf. This person is referred to as "the surrogate decision maker" or "health-care proxy." If you want your advance directive to be effective you *must* talk to the person who will make decisions on your behalf as well as the person you have designated as alternative decision maker (if the first person is unable to fill that position when needed) to make sure that both understand your wishes *and are willing* to follow them.

Sometimes the most obvious person to serve as surrogate decision maker isn't necessarily the best choice. A loving husband or wife or an adult son or daughter can't always make the decision to stop treatment even in the knowledge that it is what their loved one would want. This inability can arise from an overwhelming (if unreasonable) sense of guilt or simply from being crippled by the responsibility of making the decision that could hasten death. In some cases, surrogate decision makers have religious or philosophical objections to what their loved ones want and with the legal authority to make decisions on that person's behalf now choose a different route. Legally, the surrogate is obligated to follow the written instructions of the patient, but in reality, hospitals can be reluctant to defy a family member's decisions, especially if it means going to court. You should choose a surrogate and alternate *very* carefully and talk at length about what is written down in the living will and about your values, what you fear the most, and what you hope can happen when death is near. Although the living will form for your state should be followed, without a surrogate this form, with a series of boxes to check, may not adequately guide the medical team's decisions about your care.

Problems can also arise, especially in the form of family disagreement if one designates more than one person to serve as surrogate decision maker. Multiple decision makers who disagree with one another lessen the possibility that the patient's wishes will be honored and increase the possibility of tension among family members. The surrogate decision maker is so critical to ensuring that a person's wishes are honored that some people choose to have a surrogate with no written instructions. In such a case, one needs to be certain the surrogate understands and will follow one's preferences and values for end-of-life care. If there is a completely trustworthy friend or family member who knows what you want ("She will paint my nails" one woman said about the friend she chose to be her surrogate) and who has a thorough understanding of your values, this may be the right approach. Clear instructions should be given on the advance directive that you are designating a surrogate and giving that person all rights to make decisions on your behalf.

If possible, it would also be a good idea if members of your family know that this is the decision you have made. In fact, it's always a good idea to tell family members after you have designated a surrogate. Husbands and wives sometimes assume they are the designated decision maker; hurt feelings and anger aimed at the medical team can result when they find they are not. The same is true when particular adult children or siblings assumes that surely they have been designated the decision maker and are devastated and angry on finding this is not the case. While it may be difficult to tell family members who expect to be the designated surrogate that they are not, it's far better to have that conversation in advance of a medical emergency if at all possible than risk family members falling into arguments when you can no longer speak for yourself. Of course, it's possible that the very reason that leads someone not to choose a husband or wife or a particular son or daughter is also the reason no conversation is possible with the person, who will be angry when discovering someone else was designated. The better part of wisdom is to talk to family members *if at all possible*.

Filing the Advance Directive. Not letting people know where the advance directive is filed or filling it out too long ago can also result in a person's wishes not being honored. Many people believe that once they've filled out the document and filed it in a safe place, the task is over, even if completed years ago. But if you fill out an advance directive and file it with your lawyer or with your papers at home and no one else knows where it is, the advance directive will not be available when you can no longer speak for yourself. Or if the advance directive was filled out too long ago, it may no longer be useful when needed. A ten-year-old advance directive is not likely to help guide medical care; it will almost certainly be rejected because too many things will have changed for the patient: age, medical condition, and appropriate surrogate perhaps being the most important.

As Zitter says, planning for end-of-life care, including filling out an advance directive, is not "a one-stop shop." Such plans require "ongoing reflection and communication."[18] People often change their minds about what kind of condition they could tolerate when facing a life-threatening illness. Even a two-year-old advance directive may be considered out of date if the circumstances of the patient between the time it was completed and the time of admission to a hospital have changed dramatically. Ideally people should revisit their advance directive yearly and most certainly prior to a planned hospital stay. Also, when being admitted to the hospital, just answering yes when asked if you have a living will and giving it to the hospital to be put in your file may not be sufficient. Go over the advance directive with your surrogate prior to being hospitalized (or after you are admitted if it is an unexpected hospital stay) and review it with someone on staff, making sure your living will has been included in your record. Also, be aware that an advance directive cannot typically be housed in the hospital's records after leaving the hospital and still be considered active. Once a patient has left the hospital, the advance directive will be filed somewhere with permanent hospital documents and will most likely not show up in the patient's active file if the patient is readmitted. While there are efforts to make patient records more readily and consistently available—for instance with digital files—many hospitals do not yet have that capacity. Patients or their surrogates need to be proactive regarding the existence of a living will and make sure health-care providers are aware of it at the appropriate time.

Options 1 and 2. Another serious problem that keeps advance directives from being effective when needed is a lack

of awareness regarding what it means when you check the first
or second option on the form. Many forms begin with these
instructions:

> Initial ONE of the following two statements with which
> you agree:
>
> ___ I direct that all medically appropriate measures be pro-
> vided to sustain my life regardless of my physical or
> mental condition.
>
> ___ There are circumstances in which I would not want
> my life to be prolonged by further medical treatment.
> In these circumstances, life-sustaining measures should
> not be initiated and if they have been, they should be
> discontinued. I recognize that is likely to hasten my
> death. In the following, I specify the circumstances
> in which I would choose to forego life-sustaining
> measures.

The problem with option 1, which indicates that everything "medically appropriate" be done, resides in the ambigu-
ous meaning of "medically appropriate." When does a measure
become medically *in*appropriate if one checks this box? As
noted at the beginning of the first chapter, there is always more
that can be done even when it is likely only to prolong death
and perhaps make death more agonizing. Providing all medically appropriate measures can lead to a great deal of care—
much of it ineffective in prolonging life in any meaningful
way and perhaps creating and prolonging agony in dying. In
checking the option-1 box, you need to consider what a meaningful prolongation of life means to you. What I would find
intolerable, someone else may prefer to death. If patients do
check that box, they need to let surrogate decision makers and
other family members know what to do everything medically
appropriate means to them.

By way of example, Jessica Zitter describes an elderly man
who had written, "I want you to do EVERYTHING in your
power to keep me alive AS LONG AS YOU POSSIBLY
CAN!"[19] So even when Vincent was unconscious, except for an

occasional indication of being in pain when turned, his doctors followed his directive by inserting a breathing tube and sewing a tube into his stomach and another into his bladder. Powerful antibiotics were necessary but not entirely successful in treating the bacteria that covered his body. Because of these resistant bacteria, he had to be "isolated from the world of the living," Zitter says. "He would never again feel the touch of human skin on his body, just the clammy latex of a disposable glove and the brush of a paper gown."[20] Finally, on his last admission, Vincent's body was breaking down, with his skin and muscle deteriorating until his hip socket was actually visible. Is it likely this is what the patient had in mind when he wrote clear orders to "do everything in your power to keep me alive"? Zitter doesn't think so:

> I am sure that Vincent could not have known what he was setting himself up for when he wrote that note. He could never have imagined that, with our fancy treatments, we could keep his body going even while it was trying its hardest to die. And now he was suffering mightily, with all of the grit drained from his body.[21]

Patients have the right to check the first box, directing that all medically appropriate measures be provided to sustain life regardless of physical or mental condition. Those who for a variety of reasons don't trust the medical community may find peace in checking this box. As mentioned in chapter 2, many African Americans fall within this group in part because of their mistrust of the medical system. But before checking it, people need to be educated regarding what that may mean, and they need to be clear about what they intend and let their surrogate and other family members know.

There can also be problems regarding the second option. Checking a series of boxes may not adequately guide the medical team's decisions about your care. Checking the boxes may, for instance, be too vague to address an unexpected situation. On the other hand, the instructions can be overly specific and therefore tie the medical team's hands in light of unforesee-able medical circumstances. No one can foresee every possible medical situation and state clearly what one would wish under every potential circumstance. This is, again, another good reason to have a well-informed and trustworthy surrogate decision maker. Fill out the form, but make sure there is someone who can interpret it according to your wishes and values.

Following State Laws. To ensure that an advance directive will be effective you should know and follow the laws regulating advance directives in the state in which you live. Jessica Zitter gives an example of a contentious family situation where someone had been clearly designated as surrogate decision maker but the advance directive had not been properly notarized as required in that particular state. (Not all states require notarization, but some do.) Family members began to argue over who had the right to make a decision, and in the end, the patient's wishes were overlooked and the opportunity for meaningful good-byes was lost.[22] Filling out your advance directive and filing it with your lawyer can ensure that state laws have been followed. But remember that while filing your living will with your lawyer—if you have one—may be a good idea, it is not necessary. Don't wait until you can afford a lawyer or until you find the time to make an appointment. Your state's requirements for a living will and the form itself can be found online. You can follow those requirements without the aid of a lawyer if you don't have one.

Finally, remember that filling out an advance directive has nothing to do with physician-assisted death. You cannot ask a family member or medical staff to do something that is illegal. Equally important is knowing that simply having an advance directive will not be interpreted to mean that you want the medical team to be less rigorous in your care. *A living will is a means of communication.* Hence, in addition to the boxes checked, it is important to indicate your values and what you fear the most or most hope will happen at the end of life in a written and signed document that you share with your surrogate and include with your living will. For instance, everyone is afraid of gasping for breath or experiencing pain, but it may be important if you note what your worst fear is.

ORGAN DONATION

Living-will forms typically include an indication of whether one wants to be an organ donor at death. The Department of Motor Vehicles (DMV) also asks people renewing their driver's licenses if they want to be an organ donor; a positive response is indicated on the license itself. While including one's desire to be an organ donor at death on the living will and on a driver's license is important, signing the national organ registry, which can be found online, will help ensure that your wish is honored. There is a significant disparity between those who say they support organ donation (90 percent in one survey) and those who actually register or who agree to donate the organs of a loved one (about 45 percent are registered).[23] As a result of this disparity, about 20 people of the 120,000 waiting for an organ die every day (7,300 every year) while waiting for a transplant. While stating the number of people who are dying because of a shortage of organs may be impressive, perhaps a stronger motivation for indicating you want to be an organ donor is to consider it positively. One person whose organs are donated at death can save up to eight lives and improve the lives of up to fifty people.

There are common misconceptions regarding organ donation that keep some people from signing the national registry or indicating on an advance directive and driver's license that they want to be a donor. Probably the most common misconception, especially among groups who already mistrust the medical profession, is fear that EMTs and medical staff in the hospital will be less likely to revive you once they find you are an organ donor and may even declare you dead prematurely. In fact, extra care is taken to make sure a person is brain dead (or, in some cases, dead with the cessation of heartbeat) when known to be an organ donor. Also, after death has been pronounced, it is not hospital staff who procure the organs but an independent organ-procurement team. There are fifty-eight such organizations in the United States, and each is a member of the Organ Procurement and Transplantation Network, a federally mandated network overseen by the United Network for Organ Sharing. While many people remember news stories about famous and wealthy people being sent to the top of an organ-donation list, these stories may or may not have been true at the time, and now such a practice is clearly prohibited. A protocol has long been in place prohibiting people from receiving organs because they are well known, make public appeals, or are wealthy.

Many people believe that you cannot be a donor if you are sick or well beyond middle age. In truth, while some organs may be nonviable because of disease or age, each donor's organs are evaluated for whether they can be used. Perhaps an older person's corneas are no longer usable, but the bone marrow may be. Also, some people are concerned that the religious institution to which they belong may prohibit organ donation, when in reality only a few religions have made declarations against it. Furthermore, people who expect to have an open-casket funeral or viewing prior to a funeral can be assured that organ donation does not prohibit this practice. And a donor's family is never charged for the retrieval of organs. In considering the ethics of resisting and accepting death, we need to remember that in accepting our own mortality and making preparations for what we hope will happen when we die, we can resist death for others whose lives can be saved or enhanced because we decided to be an organ donor.

POLST

POLST is an acronym for the rather awkward string of words that designate a protocol for Practitioner Orders for Life-Sustaining Treatment. Some states use a slightly different acronym: MOLST (Medical Orders for Life-Sustaining

Treatment), MOST (Medical Orders for Scope of Treatment), and POST (Physician Orders for Scope of Treatment), but they all mean generally the same thing. However clumsy the phrase, POLST, which is a legal document for patients with an advanced illness, marks a significant improvement in ensuring that a seriously ill patient's goals of care, in the event of a medical emergency, are known—and followed.[24] Unlike an advance directive, POLST *requires* a conversation between a health-care provider and a patient:

> During the conversation, the patient discusses his or her values, beliefs, and goals for care, and the health care professional presents the patient's diagnosis, prognosis, and treatment alternatives, including the benefits and burdens of life-sustaining treatment. Together they reach an informed decision about desired treatment, based on the person's values, beliefs and goals for care.[25]

Nurse practitioners, physicians' assistants, and social workers can fill out the form, although it requires the physician's signature. It also differs from a living will in that it is portable—that is, the POLST form accompanies a patient from one institution, such as a hospital, to another, such as a rehab or nursing facility. But also, unlike an advance directive, POLST is not intended for use by every patient. It is not a form you can fill out in advance of a serious illness, and it does not substitute for naming a surrogate decision maker. While it does not require a prognosis of impending death, it is intended for use by someone who is seriously ill and whose death may possibly be imminent within the year. It is, in fact, the seriousness of a patient's condition that makes standing orders desirable.

Leslie Kernisan, a physician who promotes the use of POLST, especially for elderly patients, identifies three pitfalls that keep a POLST form from being effective. The first is "signing POLST without adequate conversation and input from clinicians," which can happen when an institution encourages a patient to fill out a POLST form but fails to make arrangements to talk to a health-care provider. This, of course, undermines the purpose of the form, which is to set goals of care and make them known to a member of the medical team. In this case a patient or family member needs to insist on talking to the appropriate person. Before they have that conversation, Kernisan suggests that patients and their families be prepared by reviewing the basics of advance-care planning, which she describes in four steps. Her advice is appropriate for writing a living will as well:

1. Understand health conditions and how they are likely to progress
   —Hope for the best, prepare for likely crises/declines
2. Articulate values and preferences for future care
   —Include designating a surrogate decision-maker
3. Document in writing
4. Re-assess preferences and plans periodically[26]

Kernisan also says that patients should keep in mind that they can always ask a doctor to discuss a POLST form that has already been signed.

A second pitfall is not being able to find the POLST form at the moment it is needed. Even though the form is meant to follow a patient from one institution to another, in an emergency this does not always occur. Some states have better systems for sharing patient information than others. Kernisan encourages patients and their families to be proactive in making sure the POLST has been made available to health-care providers when a patient moves from one institution to another. This advice highlights the fact that while it shouldn't be necessary for patients to have an advocate—a family member or friend who can speak up for them—it often is. The advocate, however, shouldn't assume the role of antagonist. Making enemies of the health-care team is not a good idea. But the family member or friend should be alert to what is happening—or not happening—and be willing to speak up if necessary.

The third reason POLST is not always effective is that patients do not always revise the form after their health changes. Kernisan, for example, describes a patient who seemed near death, and the POLST was at hand with DNAR orders. The patient improved unexpectedly, but the POLST wasn't updated to fit the new situation. When the patient was hospitalized again, there was confusion regarding whether the previous form still expressed the patient's wishes. As with the advance directive, people should review the POLST form regularly and most certainly when their health changes or a hospital visit is required or has ended.

Advance directives and POLST are not perfect vehicles for ensuring that a patient's wishes for end-of-life care will be honored, but they are extremely important, especially if one views them as a means of communication. As pointed out in the introduction, there are many reasons why we don't talk about death: simple procrastination, superstition and our own fear of death, or concern that we will upset family members. But the cost of not talking about death can be enormous. Studies show that most people are more afraid of dying than they are of death itself. Almost the only way to address our fear is to talk about what we want and put it in writing.

TALKING ABOUT DEATH

Because it is difficult for most people to talk about death, a number of resources have been made available to help people initiate such conversations. Apart from reading these resources, people might consider identifying appropriate occasions to talk about their own deaths and encourage family members to do the same. For example, specific events such as filling out a living will or experiencing the death of someone we love can prompt conversation among family members. Having a conversation with older individuals about planning for end-of-life care could start by asking what it was like when their parents, or siblings, or spouses died. Many older people will have stories about the death of a loved one and will be eager to share them, including what was especially unpleasant or what was most positive, what they regret or what they appreciate. This conversation can offer a segue into asking, "What would you like to happen when you may be near death?" Similar opportunities can arise for talking to family members of any age. A severe illness or a funeral of a family member can provide an appropriate time to talk about what others would want if such a thing happened to them.[27]

There are also resources to help families, friends, and church members talk about death. *My Gift of Grace: A Conversation Game for Living and Dying Well* was developed when the obituary of a ninety-three-year-old woman asked that people contribute to a Kickstarter project for a card game her grandson, Jethro Heiko, was developing for his Philadelphia-based design firm to help people talk about death:

> *My Gift of Grace* is a game that helps families and friends talk about death and dying. . . . This is a project that can help us prepare ourselves for life's endings and to live our lives with greater grace and resilience, two qualities which Rhoda embodied throughout her life.[28]

The game (which costs about $30) includes cards divided into questions, activities, and statements. Some questions are, as one would expect, about one's wishes at the end of life, such as question 11 ("In order to provide you with the best care possible, what three nonmedical facts should your doctor know about you?") and question 15 ("What music do you want to be listening to on your last day alive?"). There are also questions regarding one's funeral: "If only one story is told at your memorial service what would you want it to be?" Not all of the questions, however, are focused on death. Question 42, for instance, asks, "Think of the last time you got angry with someone you loved. What did you do?" Activity cards vary from visiting a local cemetery and talking to someone who works there to writing New Year's resolutions. Statement cards include "I'm concerned about being a burden on my family." There are rules to the game, but for those who aren't interested in playing by the rules, the cards can simply be used as conversation starters, and ones that people aren't interested in can be skipped.

The Death Over Dinner program has become a popular way to encourage people to talk about death. When Michael Hebb was fourteen, he lost his father to Alzheimer's. When he was thirty, he was alarmed to find that only 25 percent of people die outside of hospitals whereas 75 percent wish they could die at home and that a majority of bankruptcies occur because of expenses related to end-of-life care. He thought that the way Americans experience death "was the most important and costly conversation America was not having."[29] Hence was born Death Over Dinner, which has become an international movement gathering over 70,000 people to discuss death while having dinner with family and friends.[30]

One of the best set of resources for helping you discuss end-of-life care with the person who will serve as your surrogate is offered by the Commission on Aging and Dying and can be found online for free.[31] There are ten tools, perhaps the most useful being the seventh one: the Proxy Quiz for Family or Physicians. Here your health-care proxy fills out a questionnaire in the way she or he thinks you would answer the question. People who think they know each other extremely well have found that they often get something wrong, such as indicating "fear of being a financial burden on loved ones" as the worst fear when in reality their loved one's worst fear is being in pain or having limited awareness.

Not all these tools, games, or events will be right for everyone. Some people won't need to find outside sources to help them talk to their loved ones, but most of us need encouragement. Allen Verhey's suggestion that such conversations could occur at church is worth considering. People not only need to be educated about filling out advance directives and POLST but also would welcome discussing death in the context of their faith. It might also offer an opportunity for interfaith conversation. Members of the Christian, Muslim, and Jewish communities could share their respective traditions' beliefs and practices and encourage people to talk about their personal beliefs, fears, and hopes about death and dying.

QUESTIONS FOR REFLECTION

1. Can you describe a relationship you've had with a physician that is consistent with any of the three types described here: paternalistic (hierarchical), informative (egalitarian), or interpretative (reciprocal responsibility)? Which do you think you prefer?
2. Do you have an advance directive? Does anyone other than you know where it is? Are you confident that the surrogate decision maker you have chosen knows your wishes and will be able to carry them out?
3. Do you hope to be an organ donor when you die? If so, have you signed the national registry?
4. If you have experienced the death of someone close to you, can you remember how you expressed your grief to others as well as the best and the worst things people said to you?

5

Funerals, Burial, and Grief

Caitlin Doughty is a mortician who runs a nonprofit funeral home, "Undertaking LA," in Los Angeles. She is also founder of the Order of the Good Death, which includes members from the funeral industry, artists, and academics who are exploring ways to encourage people who live in "a death-phobic culture" such as ours to talk about and prepare for death, including what they want done with their bodies after they die. In her new, fascinating, and often-humorous book about how various cultures prepare and dispose of the bodies of those who are diseased, she asks why our culture is so squeamish when it comes to talking about death:

> Why do we refuse to have these conversations, asking our family and friends what they want done with their body when they die? Our avoidance is self-defeating. By dodging the talk about our inevitable end, we put both our pocketbooks and our ability to mourn at risk.[1]

Doughty wants to reform the funeral industry of which she is a part by making it less profit oriented, more ecologically friendly, and more open to families being involved in tending to their loved one's body.

This final chapter will explore how bodies are treated in funeral practices and how we mourn today compared to the nineteenth century. Since each era presents strengths as well as weaknesses, comparing them may help us discern what we believe could be best practices today. It also describes current traditional burial and cremation practices and alternatives that are being explored. After offering reflections on planning one's own funeral, the chapter concludes with reflections on how we live with grief and what we should and shouldn't say to someone who is grieving.

FUNERAL AND MOURNING
PRACTICES: THEN AND NOW

There are two significant differences in the way people in the nineteenth century conducted funerals and expressed their grief and the way we react to death in the United States today. First, in the nineteenth century, viewings and funerals were held at home in the parlor or "death room." Members of the family prepared the body; embalming, which was used on Civil War battlefields to bring fallen soldiers' bodies back to their families, was not typically used for home viewings. In the twentieth century and continuing today, viewings and funerals moved to funeral homes—sometimes called funeral parlors decorated to mimic the parlors from people's homes. Trained morticians prepare the body for viewing and burial. Embalming became more popular in the twentieth century, and today it is usually required by funeral homes if the body is to be viewed.

Second, grief was expressed more visibly, especially by the way upper-class women dressed in the nineteenth century, and for a longer period of time. In spite of this outward display of grief, women who were in mourning were kept isolated from society. Today, once the funeral is over, there is little in the way people dress that tells the world someone is grieving. Furthermore, people who mourn are expected to return rather quickly to their daily routines outside the home. Hence, the nineteenth century provided the freedom to express one's grief through visible signs of mourning, but it also imposed strict expectations of how one should behave, with little choice to do otherwise. In contrast, the twenty-first century provides freedom from strict social mores regarding how we grieve, but it also discourages us from expressing our grief more openly, even if that is what we would prefer to do.

Wakes and a House in Mourning. In the nineteenth century, the "wake," which we often refer to as the "viewing" today, took place at home in the parlor or death room for one to four days. The length of time had at least two practical purposes: First, it gave time to make sure the person was indeed dead and didn't, therefore, wake up from what turned out to be a deep sleep. It also allowed relatives to come from distances that required a few days' travel. The home itself was arranged for death. Clocks were stopped at the time of death; black veils covered mirrors; and flowers and candles were set out to mask the odor of death at a time when embalming was not commonly used. Black ribbons or a black wreath were hung on the outside door to alert people that a death had occurred in the family. Photographing the deceased was also a common practice, in a coffin or with the body posed, sometimes with loved ones, to make it look more alive.

While all these practices emphasized the stark reality that a death had occurred, some were based on superstitions. A mirror may have been covered to keep the spirit of the dead from being trapped inside it; photographs of family members were sometimes placed face down to keep the spirit from inhabiting those bodies whose photographs were on display; and the casket was removed from the house feet first, preventing the deceased from "looking back" and causing the death of another person. We shouldn't, however, think that all people in the nineteenth century believed their homes could be threatened by the spirit of the person who had died. Some of these practices remained in place simply because they were tradition, and sometimes their meaning changed. For instance, when a funeral procession passed one's house, curtains were closed so that the deceased couldn't "see" you looking out the window and mark you as the next one to die. This tradition, however, began to be interpreted differently by some people who simply closed their curtains on such occasions out of respect for the grieving family—not wanting them to feel that they were being gawked at.

In the twentieth century, many of these practices were not only given new meanings but were set aside altogether. When viewings were moved away from the home, turning the home parlor or death room into the "living room," the body was sent to a "funeral home" or "funeral parlor," which is even now often decorated to look something like someone's living room. And while hanging a black wreath on the door or decorating the home with black cloth may have served the positive purpose of letting neighbors know that a family was in grief, today there are few ways a family can publicly indicate it is in mourning; trying to recover the practices from the nineteenth century would probably resemble Halloween decorations more than symbols for mourning the dead.

Photographing the dead isn't as popular as it was in the nineteenth century, but it does still exist and can provide comfort, especially to families who have lost an infant. According to their website, an organization calling itself Now I Lay Me Down to Sleep "trains, educates, and mobilizes professional-quality photographers to provide beautiful heirloom portraits to families facing the untimely death of an infant." Although the name may strike some as overly sentimental, the service that Now I Lay Me Down to Sleep provides can be significant after a stillbirth or when a child dies soon after birth. Apart from using the service of professional photographers, a family member may photograph a child who is lost at birth. The baby who was stillborn or who died shortly after birth is often given a name and continues to be considered a son or daughter and sibling. The photograph may continue to be displayed, even if not prominently, serving to show that "there was a child."[2]

Announcing a Death. Letting family members know that someone had died posed challenges in the days before telephones. Often one had to rely on letters, which could be slow to be delivered. In my family, we found a handwritten letter from 1889 that includes the stark statement "I was glad to hear from you but sorry to hear that Mother was dead." Far from being as callous as that line initially seems, the letter is both poignant and compassionate as the woman who wrote the letter was asking her sister to come live with her because they were the last living relatives from their generation in their family. ("They are all gone but you and me.") The matter-of-fact opening line can most likely be explained by the considerable amount of time that had passed since their mother had died and the letter announcing her death had been received. Of course obituaries were also used, and toward the end of the nineteenth century some people had access to telephones, but news could be slow to arrive for those who were far away.

Today, letting people know that a death has occurred is typically not a problem. Telephone, e-mail, and Facebook can be used to let many people know quickly when someone has died, and in the case of e-mail and Facebook, people can express their grief to one another as a group soon after a death has occurred. Technology can also be used to include people from far away in a funeral. My husband and I sat in New Jersey and watched the live video feed of a funeral in South Africa as we mourned the sudden death of a good friend. We felt enormous comfort seeing our friends gathered for the service and hearing firsthand the statements from family members, friends, and the pastor. It wasn't the same as being physically present, but we felt that we were attending the service nonetheless.

But even as modern technology can bring us together when someone dies, it presents its own set of problems. While some people want to share photos on Facebook of loved ones on their deathbeds, others find such postings intrusive and disturbing. Also, people have been known to announce a death on Facebook before the family has been able to break the news to the appropriate people in a more personal way. And there are instances of Facebook announcements of someone's death posted in error or sometimes as a prank.

There is also the problem of what to do with someone's

Facebook page after that person has died. You should consider setting your Facebook page to indicate whether you want your account to be deleted or to become a memorialized page after you die. (Facebook must receive a legitimate request to change a deceased person's Facebook page to a memorialized page along with documentation that certifies the person has died.[3]) A legacy contact can also be named by going to "settings" on your Facebook page. The person you name can manage your account after you are gone. Without taking these steps, people can receive Facebook notices from the Facebook account of someone who has passed away, which can be very upsetting to family and friends, and some people continue to tag a friend or family member when making posts on their own Facebook pages long after the person has died.

How do we decide what is appropriate? Rules for Facebook etiquette can be found online to guide people who use Facebook in how to connect with others when someone is dying or has already passed away.[4] In the twenty-first-century United States, however, rules of etiquette may simply carry no weight. Unlike our nineteenth-century counterparts, we have entered a time in our culture when doing things our own way without being restricted by rules of etiquette tends, for good or ill, to rule the day.

Mourning. Nineteenth-century social mores dictated a long and public display of mourning for upper- and middle-class women. Queen Victoria, who wore mourning cloths for over forty years after her husband, Prince Albert, died in 1861, set the standard that made its way to the United States. When Wendy in J. M. Barrie's 1902 novel *Peter Pan* had been in Neverland for quite some time she remarked, "Mother must be in half mourning by now." Barrie's character was referring to one of the three stages of grief that governed mourning practices at the time, including how women—and to a far lesser extent men—were expected to dress and behave for each stage of mourning. These rules applied most strictly to women who had lost their husbands and were modified for mourning the death of a child or other family members.

The first stage of mourning was called deep or heavy mourning. Widows were required not only to wear black clothing but also black jewelry, veils, and bonnets (rather than hats). To accentuate the expression of grief, black crape covered a woman's clothing and draped over her bonnet to cover her face. Although a woman's grief was publicly acknowledged through her clothing, she was for the most part secluded during the first year after her husband's death. Widows in the first stage of mourning didn't speak to people in public other than family and friends, and they didn't attend social gatherings. It is why neighbors were outraged when the character Scarlet O'Hara danced in her "widow's weeds" in *Gone with the Wind*.

Deep mourning could last a year or longer for a widow and was followed by "second mourning." For the next nine to twelve months, black collars and cuffs were replaced with white, veils were still worn but shortened, lace could be added to clothing, and a wider variety of jewelry could be worn. The third and last stage was called "half mourning"—the stage Wendy referred to in *Peter Pan* in reference to her mother's thinking that she had lost her children. Black clothing could be exchanged for gray or even muted colors, such as lilac, lavender, or mauve, and simple cloth could be replaced with fabric that included a pattern. Half mourning lasted about six months. In all, mourning for a woman who lost her husband lasted about two-and-a-half years. As each stage came to an end, her clothing changed, and she was gradually able to join social functions again.

Expectations for a grieving husband were not elaborate, but there were ways in which a man's dress indicated that he had lost his wife. He wore a dark suit, black crape around his hatband, and perhaps a black armband. (Even babies are sometimes photographed wearing a black armband.) Unlike women, men were allowed—and perhaps even expected—to remarry soon after a wife's death, especially if they had children who needed to be cared for at home. In such cases, the new wife might wear mourning clothes to honor the death of her husband's previous wife. Rules of etiquette for mourning the deaths of family members other than a husband or wife were also specific. Mourning the death of a parent or a child over ten lasted between six months and a year. Mourning children under ten lasted three to six months. Siblings were mourned for six to eight months, grandparents for six months, cousins for six to twelve weeks, and more distant relatives and friends were mourned for three weeks or more.

These elaborate rules regarding mourning had positive and negative effects on people's lives. On the one hand, people who had experienced a significant loss could display visible signs to indicate that they were mourning a loved one. There was also recognition that sorrow over losing someone we love lasts a long time. Men had to return to work, but women who didn't work weren't expected to resume their daily routines for quite a long while. These expectations, however, could also be overly strict and unwelcome. Anyone watching the British TV series *Downton Abby* may remember Mary's being relieved to hear that she didn't have to go into "full mourning" when her fiancé perished in the Titanic because the engagement had not yet been announced. The fictional account of Scarlet O'Hara dancing in her "widow's weeds" no doubt represented women in real life—perhaps especially those who were young—who did not want to spend two years secluded from society while they mourned the death of their husbands. Furthermore, women who had been the victims of abusive husbands surely did not want to grieve their husbands' deaths for a year or two, remaining as isolated as their marriages may already have forced them to be.

One also needs to note that these elaborate mourning practices were clearly intended for wealthy women who could afford the various forms of mourning clothes and who did not have to work. Less wealthy women bought secondhand mourning clothes or dyed some of their regular clothes black, but they did not have the luxury of refraining from work. And, of course, it was an entirely different story for slaves living in the first half of nineteenth-century America. Slaves were sometimes allowed to participate in their own rituals regarding the dead, including some that originated in Africa and the Caribbean, such as placing personal items belonging to the person who had died on a grave, but there were no elaborate clothes to wear and certainly no expectation that work would cease. No wonder so many people over the years have railed against and finally rejected rules of etiquette regarding mourning and resist any new impositions of such rules today. Expectations governed by etiquette could restrict women's movements beyond what an individual actually wanted, and they applied only to women who could afford to follow them and who were free to do so.

Today, etiquette regarding mourning clothes has changed dramatically. Even though many women still wear black to funerals, wearing the color once favored by the person who died is gaining popularity. Hence, the actress Sarah Jessica Parker can be seen photographed in a black dress with pink shoes as she emerged from a car to attend the funeral of the comedian Joan Rivers, who loved the color pink. Our daughter wore a red blouse to my mother's graveside-memorial service because red had been her grandmother's favorite color—a preference she had expressed even in the days leading up to her death. Our son wore a black sweater with blue jeans rather than the once-mandatory suit, a way of dress that matched his style—casual but dignified—and that my mother would have appreciated. But even though we have moved away from the strict rules of etiquette required of wealthy women and to a lesser extent men in the nineteenth century, there are unwritten rules or at least expectations in current U.S. society that can also have detrimental effects. Perhaps it was excessive to require nineteenth-century upper-class women to wear black and stay at home for such an extended period of time, and as noted, etiquette regarding dress applied only to free women who could afford to follow them. But now the expectation is that one will bounce back quickly after a funeral. People would deem it odd if black clothes were worn days and weeks after a death, even though the person in grief may simply not feel like wearing bright clothing. And people today are expected to return to work or other activities outside the home very soon after the funeral. While some people welcome these activities as a distraction, others would covet remaining isolated for a while. What are best practices for mourning today? Society may never agree on standard rules of etiquette again, but we may nevertheless want to consider what we believe is appropriate.

BURIAL AND CREMATION:
TRADITIONAL PRACTICES AND NEW OPTIONS

Years ago, I knew a woman whose husband died suddenly. As a couple barely past middle age, they had found no reason to talk about their wishes at death and had never made any plans regarding what the surviving spouse should do when one of them died. Hence the wife, suddenly a widow, found herself needing to purchase a coffin and cemetery plot and plan her husband's funeral as she moved about in the haze of unexpected grief. As a result of her experience, my husband and I bought a cemetery plot where we can bury up to five cremains. Neither of us nor any member of our family will have to turn attention to purchasing a burial plot or wonder if we want traditional cremation or burial. Some people even purchase a headstone while they are still alive, leaving it blank until the time comes to record someone's death. If you aren't prepared to go that far in planning, it is at least important for you to write down your wishes to guide your family in how you hope your body will be taken care of in death.

One of the most important things you should indicate in writing is whether you prefer cremation or more traditional burial. Whether one has already made that decision or not, most of us need to examine the details of cremation and burial more carefully to understand exactly what each entails.

Traditional Burial. While some Christian funerals still occur in the sanctuary of a church, many more are held at a funeral home. While states regulate many of the laws about burial, what is legal according to state law may not be allowed according to the policies of funeral homes or cemeteries. Knowing what these policies are will help you make decisions that can be honored; they will also help the family know what to expect. Embalming, for instance, is not required by law if the body is to be buried within twenty-four hours and refrigeration is available, but many funeral homes require embalming if there is to be a viewing beforehand or an open casket at the service. Also, except in Michigan and Louisiana, the state does not mandate the use of the outer liner or vault for burial, which is typically made of concrete, steel, or fiberglass, but many cemeteries require one. The outer liner serves several purposes. It makes it easier for the cemetery caretakers to mow the lawn because it prevents the ground from sinking as the casket and body deteriorate. It also ensures that when a new grave is dug, no other body will have shifted from its grave to the new one and be uncovered in the process. It also prevents caskets and bodies from rising to the top of the ground in severe flooding.

Vaults can cost between $500 to over $15,000. Some cemeteries are offering vaultless sections, and a few small cemeteries may not require vaults at all. An average casket costs about $2,000, although they can cost as much as $30,000. A casket, however, does not have to be purchased from the funeral home. There are independent vendors that may charge less. One from a private vendor may be as little as $500 to $1,000. Cemetery plots can range from $500 to as much as $10,000 depending on the location. Don't assume, however, that all funeral-home or cemetery administrators are concerned only about selling you the most expensive package for burial. Some people have had terrible experiences, feeling that they were being manipulated in their grief to spend as much as possible, but others have found that reputable funeral homes and cemeteries are willing to work with families to purchase a package that meets their financial needs. To cut down on cost—and to make the most of limited land—some cemeteries allow two coffins to be buried on top of each other or the cremains of more than one person to be buried in one plot. Digging the grave and closing it can cost from $300 to $1,500. Some of these fees vary based on the choices one makes; others vary according to the location of the cemetery—urban vs. rural, for instance.

One of the benefits of traditional burial or of burying cremains in a traditional cemetery plot is that a gravestone marks the identity of the person who has died, providing a place for people to come to honor the dead and giving information for later generations who are researching their family's genealogy. One of the problems with burial, of course, is that we are running out of land for cemeteries. Some people are also concerned with the environmental impact of traditional burials. Because of concrete vaults with plastic liners, it could take five hundred years before the body will intermingle with the ground and achieve the state of "dust to dust."

Cremation. Cremation in modern Western society began in England in the nineteenth century and soon came to the United States. Now, for the first time in U.S. history, more people have indicated that they prefer their bodies be cremated rather than buried. There are a number of reasons for this increased preference for cremation. Many people prefer cremation to burial because it is less expensive. One can forgo the cost of embalming if there is not to be a viewing, and depending on what one wants done with the cremains, cremation doesn't require the purchase of a traditional burial plot in a cemetery. In the United States, bodies are cremated in a combustible container that may resemble a traditional casket or simply be a cardboard box. If you choose to bury the cremains in a traditional cemetery plot, you still may be required to purchase a vault or grave liner to hold the cremains. Some people find it comforting to have the ashes scattered in a place that was meaningful to the deceased, although others prefer a specific place to bury the cremains with a marker that identifies the name and dates of the person who died.

One of the most common reasons people prefer cremation has to do with time and travel required of family members who would like to attend the service. Whereas most burials are done within a few days after death, cremation allows for one to postpone the service, replacing the funeral with a memorial service weeks and sometimes months after the death. This may be of great significance for family and friends who want to attend the service but who live far away. Some people also choose cremation because they believe it is easier on the environment, for it avoids the chemicals used in embalming (unless there is a viewing) and possibly the concrete vault required in traditional burial.

One should, however, be aware that an enormous amount of energy is required to incinerate a body, and cremation causes pathogens to enter the air, mercury from people's fillings being one of the most worrisome. The cost of cremation can range from $4,000 to $6,000 if there is a service before the body is taken to the crematory. Without a service, the cost may range between $2,000 and $4,000 with the assistance of the funeral home, or $1,500 to $3,000 without the services of a funeral home. Regarding ashes that are scattered or kept in an urn at home, some people find enormous comfort in these practices while others fear that we may as a society put even more distance between ourselves and death when we can no longer roam cemeteries and read headstones of those who have gone before us.

Open-Air Cremation. Most of us tend to think of traditional burial and cremation as our only options. There are, however, alternatives either already available or being explored. Caitlin Doughty describes a very different way bodies are cremated in a small town in Colorado compared to the crematoriums most of us are familiar with. She watched the son of a woman who had died suddenly use a pickup truck to bring his mother's body to an open-air cremation site in Crestone, Colorado, right before dawn, carry her body on a cloth stretcher, and set it on the pyre. Each of the 130 mourners (almost the entire population of the town) laid a juniper bough on the woman's body. The immediate family—including a child—stacked piñon pine and spruce logs around the pyre before encircling it. Two family members came forward with torches just as the sun was coming up and lit the pyre. Prior to the cremation, volunteers from the Crestone End-of-Life project helped the woman's family and close friends prepare her body by washing her, dressing her in natural fabrics, and laying her body on a cooling blanket, which slowed down decomposition.[5] These volunteers help families and friends prepare a body at home regardless of the family's ability to pay and even if the family has chosen traditional embalming and burial or the more typical kind of cremation.

This open-air pyre uses far less fuel than traditional cremations and even significantly less wood than open-air cremations in countries like India. It is, however, not available for use to anyone other than citizens of Crestone. One woman bought a small plot of land before she died so that her body could be cremated there, and the town cremated the body of a hiker when it was found in the Crestone area months after his death, believing he had established local citizenship in death. Even though this form of cremation is thousands of years old, the open-air pyre in Crestone is the only one like it in the United States, and, in fact, there are none like it elsewhere in the Western world.[6]

Liquification. One alternative to cremation that is available and becoming increasingly popular is a liquification process that for now goes by a variety of names, such as "flameless cremation," "green cremation," or "fire to water." The chemical name of the process is alkaline hydrolysis. A machine that costs between $150,000 and $500,000 uses a chemical bath on the body that dissolves protein, blood, and fat into a dark-brown liquid. Powdery bone and metal implants are left behind. The bone can be ground into finer dust and given to the family as in traditional cremation. The liquid, which is sterile, goes into the sewer system or can be used as fertilizer.[7] The carbon footprint for liquification is significantly less than traditional cremation (about a tenth as much) because it does not use nearly the same amount of energy as required for burning bodies, and it releases no fumes into the air. It can cost less than $2,000. As of 2017, fifteen states allow this form of disposing of a body.

Recomposition, or Turning Corpses into Compost. One alternative that is now in the experimental phase will be intriguing to some and alarming to others. Katrina Spade, a thirty-seven-year-old resident of Seattle, is experimenting with how to turn human bodies into compost in what she calls the Urban Death Project. It may sound disrespectful—or out-and-out disgusting—at first hearing, but she is very serious. She is also extremely respectful of the bodies that are placed in her care as she seeks the best formula for composting bodies in the ground. Looking for an alternative to the use of formaldehyde required to preserve bodies for viewing and concerned about the diminishing land available for cemetery burial, she is also looking for an alternative to the carbon dioxide released into the air by cremation. For people who are concerned that human remains will be used to fertilize not only flowers and trees but perhaps the food we eat, Katrina Spade explains why that should not be a concern. Four to six weeks into composting, the molecules transform so that a body ceases to be human. This is why she calls this process "recomposition," an accurate and more palatable term than "composting." Farmers have been composting livestock for years and using the compost for fertilizer.

Partnering with Dr. Cheryl Johnston, who runs what most readers know as a "body farm" in North Carolina, Spade is experimenting with bodies that were donated to the Forensic Osteology Research Station (FOREST) in North Carolina.[8] Caitlin Doughty, who visited FOREST, describes two experiments that went wrong but taught them about the right—or wrong—formula. In the first case, the body was placed on and covered with woodchips, and in the second, alfalfa hay. Water was added for moisture, which encourages bacteria and microbes to enter the pile. The woodchips kept the body moist but didn't produce the nitrogen necessary to keep the body heated. The alfalfa created nitrogen but drew water away from the body, and after five months, the bones were still intact. Experiments continue with a mix of wood chips and alfalfa and the appropriate amount of water. Katrina Spade is confident that recomposition will one day be a viable alternative to burial and cremation.

Many people are understandably committed to the dignity

of traditional burial in a cemetery, with a headstone marking the identity of the person who died. Alternatives to traditional burial won't interest them. And some people find the alternatives to traditional burial and cremation disturbing. But the fact is, there will come a day when we simply will not have enough land to bury people in traditional plots. Whatever each of us chooses for ourselves or our loved ones now, considering alternatives will someday cease to be an option and become a necessity. We may want to consider whether our values about how we treat the dead can be protected in each approach to disposing of a body.

Cheryl Johnston, who runs the Forensic Osteology Research Station, accepts bodies of people who donated them prior to death for research and places them in a variety of conditions so that forensic students can study them and later perhaps determine how long ago a person died at the scene of an accident or crime. She respectfully refers to the bodies by the last names of the deceased, such as "Mr. Williams" or "Mrs. Anderson." Caitlin Doughty argues that different cultures honor their dead in a variety of ways. The day will surely come when we need to consider how to honor the dead as we find alternatives to traditional burial and cremation.

PLANNING YOUR FUNERAL

Although some people resist making plans for their own funerals, insisting that funerals are for the living, indicating our preferences can relieve family members of having to make decisions completely on their own with no guidance regarding what we would want. Writing out your wishes regarding whether you prefer cremation or burial and leaving instructions for the funeral service can take a burden from your family as they look to make decisions consistent with your tradition and values.

Body at a Funeral. Some Christian traditions always have an open casket during the service while some denominations forbid it. Without the open casket, a closed coffin has often been present at a funeral. Some people, however, believe that the body isn't necessary at the service at all. The service, they argue, is meant for the worship of God and the consolation of the living; the presence of the body of the deceased is optional. And, of course, no body is present at a memorial service. While there may be wisdom in this perspective, it seems to challenge the Christian understanding of the value of the human body as discussed in chapter 2. Tom Long insists that "funerals are about the embodied person who has died" and that "the Christian dead should be welcomed once again to their own funerals."[9] As Christians we believe in a *bodily* resurrection, which doesn't point to some disembodied human spirit that now floats in the wind. Bodies will most certainly turn to dust in this world, but we believe a recognizable "spiritual body" is resurrected to new life. At a funeral, we need to acknowledge that a real, embodied human being—a child of God—lived in this world and has died.

On the other hand, while the presence of the body may be significant, perhaps the presence of family and friends who can gather from afar for a memorial service outweighs the significance of viewing the body and of the presence of the body during the funeral. In those cases where it isn't possible to have the body present, perhaps photos of the deceased could serve as reminders of the embodied life of the person who has passed away. Through photos we can remember the real human being who existed and whose absence is now terribly painful to us. And, as Tom Long suggests, "we must summon every gift of language to establish their embodied presence in our memories and imaginations."[10]

There has often been a debate among those who think that the funeral or memorial service is to comfort the people who mourn and those who believe that it is to give witness to the resurrection. This debate, however, represents a false choice. There is no contradiction between comforting those who mourn by focusing on the memory of the person who died *and* giving witness to the resurrection. Most denominations have their own traditions and principles regarding the presence of a body and whether the casket should be open or closed as well as what is to be included in the service. In writing your instructions, you may want to consider what your denomination advises. In addition to indicating your preferences regarding whether people view your body and whether the body should be present if there is to be a funeral service, consider making your preferences known for various aspects of the service.

Bulletin. If the church allows for a choice of what should be on the cover of the bulletin (some will not), consider whether you want a personal photo on the front or a Christian symbol. If a photo, you could even include one or several to choose from in the folder with your instructions. You could also indicate the person you hope will be available to conduct the service. Also consider the form of the service. Should it include the major features of a worship service?

Music. Indicate the music you would prefer. Consider whether you believe the music should take the form of traditional hymns (indicate which are your favorites) or whether other forms of Christian music or even secular music could be included. Would you rather the congregation be asked to sing, or should music be restricted to a solo or a choir? If you are the type who thinks the decision regarding music should be left to those planning the service, consider the story of a music director who knew he was dying but refused to talk about his service. A close colleague, who knew her friend had no patience with some contemporary forms of church music, challenged him by saying, "If you don't talk to me about what music you want included in your service, I will make sure we have nothing but praise music." She herself loved praise music, but she knew her friend did not. In light of her threat, the music director finally began to talk about his preferences. Of course, the deceased will not be present to enjoy the music chosen. But the congregation and family and friends may take great comfort in recognizing hymns or praise songs that were known to be among the person's favorites and may recoil at hearing music known to be disliked by the person who died.

Prayer of Confession. Not everyone agrees that a prayer of confession belongs in a funeral. One can imagine the worst kind of guilt-inducing prayer that would push mourners deeper into despair. But a prayer of confession, carefully written, can help people express the regrets they have that can never in this lifetime be made right. A good example of a call to confession for a funeral is found in the *Book of Common Worship*:

> Let us now ask God to cleanse our hearts,
> to redeem our memories,
> and to renew our confidence in the goodness of God.

This call to confession is followed by a very general—and traditional—prayer of confession appropriate for a funeral:

> Holy God, you see us as we are,
> and know our inmost thoughts.
> We confess that we are unworthy of your gracious care.
> We forget that all life comes from you
> and that to you all life returns.
> We have not always sought or done your will.
> We have not lived as your grateful children,
> nor loved as Christ loved us.
> Apart from you, we are nothing.
> Only your grace can sustain us.
>
> Lord, in your mercy, forgive us,
> heal us and make us whole.
> Set us free from our sin,
> and restore to us the joy of your salvation
> now and forever.[11]

The prayer can, of course, be modified if the traditional language of being "nothing" and "unworthy" apart from God's grace won't sound hopeful to mourners from different traditions. But allowing people to express their regrets in a prayer of confession and then hear the proclamation of forgiveness can be a significant part of a funeral or memorial service.

Scripture. Unlike during a Sunday morning service, Scripture is often read throughout a funeral or memorial service. One often hears favorite passages that proclaim hope in Christ's victory over death. It may also be comforting if family and friends know that some of the passages being read were among their loved one's favorites. Many traditions also allow secular readings—often something meaningful to the person who died—as long as the reading doesn't contain ideas antithetical to the Christian faith, such as the two poems mentioned in chapter 2. In writing instructions for your own funeral, you could make suggestions not only for what readings could be included but also for who might step forward to read.

In light of all that has been presented so far, consider leaving a simple document with some of the following information for your family and friends to use when you die—and make sure someone knows where the document is:

1. Whether you prefer burial or cremation, and if cremation, where you want the cremains to be buried or scattered. Indicate whether you have already bought a cemetery plot or which cemetery you prefer.
2. Whether you prefer a funeral or memorial service and where you would like the service to be held.
3. What your preference is regarding the casket: type of wood, style, and how much money should be spent.
4. Which funeral home you hope will be used, if you have a preference.
5. What personal information you would like listed in the obituary. Give the correct spelling of your name, and include information about your life so that your family won't have to spend time looking up information that may be difficult to find: date and place of birth, schools you attended and degrees earned, and places where you worked. Obituaries can be expensive, but some funeral homes include placing an obituary in the newspaper as part of the funeral package.
6. Which charity you would like people to consider for a donation given in your memory.
7. What your preference is regarding floral arrangements. We had a single yellow rose in a vase for my mother who

was from Texas. Other people will appreciate a full spray for the casket made from the person's favorite flowers. Others may ask for live plants to be given to family members after the service is over.

8. Whether you want your body to be viewed prior to the service. If there is to be a viewing, do you have a preference for what you would wear?

9. Which favorite photos you particularly like or which you would hate for someone to use for display. Consider including a photo with the information you are making available to your family.

10. What your preference is for who will serve as pallbearers.

11. Which particular people you hope will speak or read during the service.

12. What favorite passages from Scripture, favorite hymns, or other types of music would you like to be used.

If you don't want to appear to be overly in control of your own funeral, you can state that these are your preferences but your family is free to make any adjustments they want. On the other hand, you may have family members whose religious views are contrary to your own, and you may want to indicate which of your wishes are to be strictly observed.

LIVING WITH GRIEF

It is part of the human condition to grieve and to grieve deeply. Our sense of loss can be overwhelming, and our grief can last a lifetime, although not typically with the same intensity as when it first arose. The longevity of grief that we seek to incorporate into our lives (rather than leave behind) marks one of the problematic aspects of Elisabeth Kübler-Ross's well-known stages of grief, which she identified in people who are dying and which are now considered part of what is experienced by people who are grieving the death of a loved one: denial, anger, bargaining, depression, and acceptance.[12]

These stages are usually interpreted to be progressive and have influenced many people who think their job is to move those who are grieving through the five stages until they reach the coveted goal of acceptance. In reality, people often move from one stage to another and back again. Anger can be expressed one day; acceptance, another; and then one may return to denial or depression. And when we are grieving the death of someone we love, the notion of acceptance does not mean that grief is gone. We learn to live with our grief, and the daily unbearable pain eases with time, but as one mother who lost her daughter recognizes, while grief can be incorporated into our lives, it does not disappear altogether:

> Now, whenever I glimpse a child with Sarah's startling blue eyes, I feel a sickening thump in my chest. Still, I rise every morning and live my life. I act nearly normal. I embrace my work, my husband and my three surviving children. Loss brought me to writing and painting. Mine is a life, filled with such little moments—at times joyful, at other times sorrowful. Not as odd a combination as some might think. They coexist within me, pleasure and sorrow, shaping who I am and how I see the world.[13]

There are no progressive stages of grief to be experienced one by one until a person reaches acceptance. While in time grief will not be as intense from day to day as it was in the beginning, a memory can bring it back. My grandmother died decades ago, but reading a letter from her when I was child that begins, "My dear little girl baby" can bring me to tears again.

Another problem with Kübler-Ross's stages of grief is what she leaves out. What about the stage of grief that occurs "after the last casserole dish is picked up—when the outside world stops grieving with you"?[14] Where does the envy of others who are not dying or who have not experienced a loss come in, and in what stage can one express guilt and remorse for hurtful actions and broken relationships that can never be resolved? Perhaps we should give up all language of "stages" when describing grief. It may certainly help people who are dying and people who mourn to know that some of what they experience has been experienced by others. At the same time, consider that "grief is as unique as a fingerprint" and "conforms to no timetable or societal expectation."[15] Believing that our job as pastor, counselor, or friend is to help someone get through the stages and find acceptance can lead us to be unintentionally insensitive to what someone is actually feeling. Our task is to be present with those we love through each phase and aspect of grief.

Lament. Against our tendency to deny the intensity of grief, there is a biblical tradition of lament that allows the individual to express anguish and anger directly to God and before the community of believers. In light of the grief brought on by death, the church can provide a space where people can express their sorrow before God and one another. Psalms of lament can assist in expressing our feelings of having been abandoned by God ("O LORD, why do you cast me off? Why do you hide your face from me?" Ps. 88:14) and our impatience with suffering ("I am weary with my moaning; every night I flood my bed with tears," Ps. 6:6). Christians tend to be uneasy with such expressions of God-forsakenness and impatience, and some respond with the overly simplistic insistence that "God never gives you more than you can bear." The psalmist knows better. Psalms of lament provide us both the permission and a vocabulary for expressing our anguish.

If psalms of lament were well known by Christian worshipers, if they were frequently read in worship, individuals would be familiar with the practice of naming the feelings that accompany grief even before a death occurs and know that they can do so in faith. Reading psalms of lament can inform individuals that they are not the first to feel abandoned by God, such as the widower who feels unbearable isolation as he locks his door and faces another evening alone or the mother who will never again see the face of her child. Can we actually bring thoughts of being abandoned *by* God *to* God in prayer? Do we dare bring those thoughts into speech before our brothers and sisters in the faith? We find the answer to those questions in Jesus' own prayer on the cross. Drawing on a psalm of lament, he cried out in anguish, "My God, my God, why have you forsaken me?" (Ps. 22:1) Why would we believe that our anguish, our despair, and our feeling that God has deserted us must never be expressed to others when Jesus himself cried out in lamentation before God?

The Bible recognizes a grief that cannot be consoled in the image of Rachel weeping for her children after the slaughter of the innocents. Rachel, in fact, "*refused* to be consoled, because they were no more" (Matt. 2:18). The tradition of lamentation allows us with Rachel to look at the world and our lives the way they really are. We are not required to face devastating events by pretending that things are not as bad as they appear when in fact things may be just as bad if not worse than appearances reveal. Lamentation also represents a bold expression of our faith because it acknowledges that there is nothing about the reality of the world or the self or life itself that cannot be brought before God, including overwhelming and even debilitating grief.

Talking about Grief. As we consider what to say—and not to say—to someone whose grief cannot be consoled, we first need to understand that we cannot fix the situation, much as we want to. We also can't run from an encounter with someone who is engulfed in such grief out of the knowledge that we don't know what to say. It's a near-impossible situation to be in. We are called to bring comfort in a situation devoid of comfort. We have to find some words to say. And we have to be willing to be quiet. We're called to be present—a "suffering presence," as Stanley Hauerwas says.[16] And while nothing we say can make the grief tolerable, some of what we say can make the grief worse. Even assurances from faith strongly held do not always bring comfort. Nicholas Wolterstorff described this situation after his adult son died alone in a climbing accident:

> Elements of the gospel which I had always thought would console did not. They did something else, something important, but not that. It did not console me to be reminded of the hope of resurrection. If I had forgotten that hope, then it would indeed have brought light into my life to be reminded of it. But I did not think of death as a

bottomless pit. I did not grieve as one who has no hope. Yet Eric was gone, *here* and *now* he is gone; *now* I cannot talk with him, *now* I cannot see him, *now* I cannot hug him, *now* I cannot hear of his plans for the future. *That* is my sorrow. A friend said, "Remember, he is in good hands." I was deeply moved. But that reality does not put Eric back in my hands now. That's my grief. For that grief, what consolation can there be other than having him back?[17]

If you say to Nicholas Wolterstorff or anyone who has experienced such a loss, "He's in a better place" or "God doesn't give us more than we can bear," you will be unintentionally cruel. These kinds of comments suggest that the unbearable grief that cannot be consoled is bearable after all and that we really should not grieve so deeply or for long.

The difficulty of the situation should make us especially mindful of not saying things that make *us* feel better but are burdensome for the one who grieves. "Let me know if there's anything I can do" may be heartfelt, but it puts a burden on the person who is grieving to come up with something. Depending on how well you know the person, you could make concrete suggestions, such as volunteering to walk the dog or weed the garden. Also, asking, "How are you doing?" represents an almost irresistible question. Besides the fact that it is a common greeting in everyday life, we really do want to know how the person is coping, and we hope it serves as an invitation for the person to express how he or she feels. We should keep in mind, however, that people often react with the socially accepted response in everyday interaction: "I'm fine." This may, in fact, be what the questioner is hoping the answer is going to be because that will make the conversation easier. We may, however, want an honest answer to "How are you really doing?" but asking the question is rarely going to result in genuine conversation. It may be the wrong time or place; you may be the wrong person at that particular moment for the one who grieves to welcome your question. The person who grieves may be barely holding things together when you ask the question that will throw her off kilter. Or, he may be enjoying the moment for the first time in a long time, when you bring him back to reality. Sometimes making a claim is better than asking a question, such as "I know this is hard for you."

There are a number of flaccid but traditional things people say, perhaps without thinking how hurtful they will be. Everyone should realize that saying, "You can always have another child" to someone who has just lost a child to miscarriage or stillbirth is cruel. The same is true with "You'll remarry someday," when said to someone who just lost a spouse. Suggesting that cherishing one's memories will bring peace fails to recognize that this person may not be ready for the loved one to be a memory. Furthermore, you don't know if difficult memories or even if remembering good things are too painful to bear.

One of the most popular things to say these days is "Everything happens for a reason." Although some Christians hold to the doctrine of special providence, believing that indeed everything that occurs happens according to God's will, this complex doctrine cannot be summarized in so simple a claim, and many Christians don't hold to special providence. The suggestion that God has orchestrated their painful loss sounds cruel to them—not comforting as the doctrine intends. And when those who do not believe in God also insist that everything happens for a reason, one wonders, *by whose hand* and to serve what purpose? Of course, some of the people who claim that everything happens for a reason also find comfort in it. One needs to be certain, however, that others will find it comforting as well.

Another popular claim that some find almost impossible to refrain from saying is "I'm sorry for your loss." However genuine, there are two problems with this claim. First, it has been overused and trivialized on TV shows. It's what every cop or detective says before interviewing someone whose loved one has just been murdered. It's what has to be said before asking the question they came to ask: "Where were you at the time of the murder?" Furthermore, some people who grieve find the claim annoying, saying it sounds too much like an apology, when the person who says it has nothing to apologize for. They want to reply, "Why are you sorry? It's not your fault."

Some people find comfort in saying, "He's in a better place," suggesting that the heavenly life is where the person belongs, but others, like Nicolas Wolterstorff, find that this does not ease their longing for the person to be present with them now. As one pastor said at a funeral, "The best place for my friend to be is right here with me." This was not intended to deny the Christian promise that in life and death we belong to God. Wolterstorff did not grieve as one who had lost hope in the resurrection; he grieved for the presence of his son then and there. Telling someone a child or spouse or friend is in a better place falls among those claims that carry an underlying message: "So you should not grieve quite so much. Things aren't as bad as you think they are."

Finally, there are things people say that are actually intended to cut off further expressions of grief rather than invite conversation: "It's been awhile since she died. Don't you think it's time you started to move on?" or "You need to pull yourself together for the sake of the kids." These questions and claims represent the inability of the questioner to bear the other's grief, and they are best left aside.

While recognizing that our affirmations cannot always bring consolation to a grieving person, we may need to distinguish between bold and honest expressions of grief and a kind of wallowing in grief over months and years that shows no assurance of Christian hope or that one's life has meaning after a loved one dies. To be sure, no parent should ever be denied the freedom to revisit the pain of having lost a child, or a widow the need to talk about the husband she still misses years later. This is one reason parents who have lost children or widows and widowers sometimes form their own social groups and meet together for years to come. No one else knows as well how much their grief lives on. But recognizing that grief can last a lifetime is not the same as living for years and decades as if the loss of a loved one means the end of one's life forever. Incorporating grief into the lives we continue to live means affirming that *we* are not dead, our own life is not over, and, in fact, God calls us into continuing purpose that may not fully assuage our grief but enables us to live with it, to reach out to others in love, and to believe that our lives continue to have meaning.

Our faith does not protect us from harm or sorrow. As Dietrich Bonhoeffer knew when he wrote from a Nazi prison, we do not believe in the god of the gaps, a god who fixes things when we face tragedy and unbearable loss. And, of course, faith does not protect us from death—our own or that of those we love. Although we know death will not have the last word, it does at least have a final word in this world for everyone who exists. In faith we seek to discern when to resist and when to accept death. In faith we comfort one another or simply sit silently when grief is beyond consolation. And when we contemplate the first question posed by the Heidelberg Confession, "What is your only comfort, in life and in death?" we respond with confidence, "That I am not my own, but belong—body and soul, in life and in death—to my faithful Savior, Jesus Christ."[18]

QUESTIONS FOR REFLECTION

1. Are there practices from the nineteenth century that you think we should try to reclaim today?
2. Do you have a preference regarding whether your body will be buried or cremated after you die? Do any of the possible alternatives—open-air cremation, liquification, or recomposition—appeal to you?
3. Have you ever considered what you believe are the essential components of a good funeral or memorial service? Do you think your family would appreciate knowing what you would prefer for your funeral, such as Scripture passages, hymns, location, and officiant?
4. Do you and your family find it difficult to talk about death? How do you think you could initiate a conversation about everyone's preferences regarding a good death?

Notes

Introduction

1. Herman Feifel, ed., *The Meaning of Death* (New York: McGraw-Hill, 1959). See also Allen Verhey, *The Christian Art of Dying: Learning from Jesus* (Grand Rapids: Wm. B. Eerdmans Publishing Co., 2011), 50–51.

2. Dudley Clendinen, "The Good Short Life," *New York Times*, Sunday Review, July 9, 2011, http://www.nytimes.com/2011/07/10/opinion/sunday/10als.html?pagewanted=all.

3. Barbara Moran, "Not Just a Death: A System Failure," *New York Times*, February 6, 2016, https://opinionator.blogs.nytimes.com/author/barbara-moran/.

4. Atul Gawande, *Being Mortal: Medicine and What Matters in the End* (New York: Henry Holt & Co., 2014), 10.

5. Haider Warraich, *Modern Death: How Medicine Changed the End of Life* (New York: St. Martin's Press, 2017), ix.

6. Jessica Nutik Zitter, *Extreme Measures: Finding a Better Path to the End of Life* (New York: Penguin Random House, 2017), xiv.

Chapter 1: Resisting and Accepting Death

1. Jessica Nutik Zitter, *Extreme Measures: Finding a Better Path to the End of Life* (New York: Penguin Random House, 2017), 32.

2. Allen Verhey, *The Christian Art of Dying: Learning from Jesus*, (Grand Rapids: Wm. B. Eerdmans Publishing Co., 2011), 14.

3. Robert Galbraith, *The Cuckoo's Calling* (New York: Little Brown & Co.), 282.

4. Verhey, *Christian Art of Dying*, 18–19.

5. Zitter, *Extreme Measures*, 31.

6. Ibid., 30–31.

7. Atul Gawande, *Being Mortal: Medicine and What Matters in the End* (New York: Henry Holt & Co., 2014), 155.

8. Zitter, *Extreme Measures*, xiii–xiv.

9. Verhey, *Christian Art of Dying*, 4.

10. Ibid.

11. See Dylan Thomas, "Do Not Go Gentle into That Good Night," https://www.poets.org/poetsorg/poem/do-not-go-gentle-good-night.

12. Gawande, *Being Mortal*, 4–5.

13. Justice Benjamin Cardoza, *Schoendorff v. Society of New York Hospital*, 105 N.E. 92 (Court of Appeals of New York), http://biotech.law .lsu.edu/cases/consent/schoendorff.htm.

14. Judge Hughes, "In the Matter of Karen Quinlan, an Alleged Incompetent," Supreme Court of New Jersey (argued January 26, 1976; decided March 31, 1976), http://law.justia.com/cases/new-jersey/supreme-court /1976/70-n-j-10-0.html.

15. Quoted by Haider Warraich, *Modern Death: How Medicine Changed the End of Life* (New York: St. Martin's Press, 2017), 77–78.

16. Jon Van, "Quinlan Case Redefined Life, Death," *Chicago Tribune*, June 13, 1985, http://articles.chicagotribune.com/1985-06-13/news /8502070415_1_karen-quinlan-life-and-death-brain-death.

17. Lee Romney, "Jahi McMath Q&A: Can Brain Death Be Reversed?" *Los Angeles Times*, January 6, 2014, http://articles.latimes.com/2014 /jan/06/local/la-me-ln-jahi-mcmath-case-questions-answers-20140106.

18. Rachel Aviv, "What Does It Mean to Die?" *The New Yorker*, February 5, 2018, https://www.newyorker.com/magazine/2018/02/05/what -does-it-mean-to-die.

19. Zitter, *Extreme Measures*, 3–6.

20. Ibid., 19–25.

21. Gawande, *Being Mortal*, 149–52, 165–70, and 172–73.

22. Warraich, *Modern Death*, 69.

23. Ibid., 80.

24. Tom L. Beauchamp and James F. Childress, *Principles of Biomedical Ethics*, 5th ed. (New York: Oxford University Press, 2001).

25. Edmund D. Pellegrino, "The Metamorphosis of Medical Ethics: A 30-Year Retrospective," *Journal of the American Medical Association* 269, no. 9 (1993): 1161.

Chapter 2: Christian Beliefs about Death

1. For an excellent description of *Ars Moriendi*, including images of the woodcuts, see Allen Verhey, "Part Two: *Ars Moriendi*," in *The Christian Art of Dying* (Grand Rapids: William B. Eerdmans Publishing Co., 2011), 77–175.

2. *The Constitution of the Presbyterian Church (U.S.A.)*, Part I, *Book of*

Confessions (Louisville, KY: Office of the General Assembly, Presbyterian Church (U.S.A.), 2016), 4.001. I am grateful to Christopher Morse for reminding me of this powerful theological affirmation from the Heidelberg Confession in his satire, *Prof. Schmoot Has Lost His Keys Again* (Eugene, OR: Wipf & Stock Publishers, 2017).

3. Thomas G. Long, *Accompany Them with Singing: The Christian Funeral* (Louisville, KY: Westminster John Knox Press, 2009), 38–39.

4. Ibid, 38.

5. Verhey, *Christian Art of Dying*, 51.

6. Ibid. 52–53. See also Elisabeth Kübler-Ross, ed., *Death: The Final Stage of Growth* (Englewood Cliffs, NJ: Prentice-Hall, 1975).

7. Verhey, *Christian Art of Dying*, 55.

8. Ibid., 51–52.

9. Ibid., 53.

10. Long, *Accompany Them with Singing*, 39.

11. Ibid., 39–40.

12. Ibid., 39. Nancy Byrd Turner, "Death Is a Door," *All Poetry*, https://allpoetry.com/Nancy-Byrd-Turner.

13. Long, *Accompany Them with Singing*, 30–31. See also Mary Elizabeth Frye, "Do Not Stand at My Grave and Weep," https://www.poemhunter.com/poem/do-not-stand-at-my-grave-and-weep/.

14. Long, *Accompany Them with Singing*, 39.

15. "U.S. Public Health Service Syphilis Study at Tuskegee," Centers for Disease Control and Prevention, last reviewed December 14, 2015, https://www.cdc.gov/tuskegee/index.html.

16. Van R. Newkirk II, "America's Health Segregation Problem: Has the Country Done Enough to Overcome Its Jim Crow Health Care History?" *The Atlantic*, May 18, 2016, https://www.theatlantic.com/politics/archive/2016/05/americas-health-segregation-problem/483219/.

17. Paul Lehmann, *Ethics in a Christian Context*, Library of Theological Ethics (Louisville, KY: Westminster John Knox Press, 2006), 74.

18. John Calvin, "Commentary on Psalm 22:4," in *Calvin's Commentary on the Bible*, https://www.studylight.org/commentaries/cal/psalms-22.html.

19. Stephen Sondheim, "No One Is Alone," from *Into the Woods* (Walt Disney Pictures, 2014), https://www.allmusicals.com/lyrics/intothewoods/nooneisalone.htm.

20. Elisabeth Kübler-Ross, *On Death and Dying: What the Dying Have to Teach Doctors, Nurses, Clergy and Their Own Families*, 40th anniversary ed. (New York: Routledge, Taylor, and Frances Group, 2009).

21. Dayna Olson-Getty, "Life-Expectancy: On Not Praying for a Miracle," *Christian Century*, September 22, 2009, 11–12. This essay is available online if you subscribe to the *Christian Century*, https://www.christiancentury.org/article/2009-09/life-expectancy.

22. Ibid.

23. Ibid.

24. W. H. Auden, *For the Time Being: A Christmas Oratorio* (Princeton, NJ: Princeton University Press, 2013). The lines quoted here can be found online, http://www.cs.utsa.edu/~wagner/church/auden/.

Chapter 3: Assisted Death and Death-with-Dignity Laws

1. Brittany Maynard, "My Right to Death with Dignity at 29," CNN.com, updated November 2, 2014, http://www.cnn.com/2014/10/07/opinion/maynard-assisted-suicide-cancer-dignity/index.html.

2. Tara Culp-Ressler, "Most Doctors in the United States Now Support 'Death with Dignity' Laws," *Think Progress*, December 17, 2014, https://thinkprogress.org/most-doctors-in-the-united-states-now-support-death-with-dignity-laws-8888c575c2ea/.

3. Josh Sanburn, "Brittany Maynard Could Revive the Stalled 'Death with Dignity' Movement, *Time*, November 1, 2014, http://time.com/3551089/brittany-maynard-death-with-dignity/.

4. In May 2018, California's End of Life Option Act was overturned by Riverside County Superior Court Judge Daniel A. Ottolia, who said that the medical-aid-in-dying act was unrelated to the purposes of the special session of the California legislature that passed it and is, therefore, unconstitutional. The law should remain in place while the decision is being appealed.

5. Ryan Anderson, "Purported Safeguards in Physician-Assisted Suicide Are Ripe for Abuse," Heritage.org, April 7, 2015, http://www.heritage.org/health-care-reform/report/purported-safeguards-physician-assisted-suicide-are-ripe-abuse.

6. Allen Verhey, *The Christian Art of Dying: Learning from Jesus* (Grand Rapids: Wm. B. Eerdmans Publishing Co., 2011), 320–21, 351.

7. Eric Metaxas, "Assisted Suicide—Like Playing God—Is Always Wrong," CNSNews.com, December 21, 2016, http://www.cnsnews.com/commentary/eric-metaxas/assisted-suicide-playing-god-always-wrong.

8. Ibid.

9. Ibid.

10. *The Constitution of the Presbyterian Church (U.S.A.)*, Part I, *Book of*

Confessions (Louisville, KY: Office of the General Assembly, Presbyterian Church (U.S.A.), 2016), 4.001.

11. Lester (Joe) Cruzan made this statement in the documentary, "The Death of Nancy Cruzan," Elizabeth Arledge, Frontline, PBS, 1992.

12. For a summary of this case, see Patricia A. King, "Dax's Case: Implications for the Legal Profession," in *Dax's Case: Essays in Medical Ethics and Human Meaning,* ed. Lonnie D. Kliever (Dallas: Southern Methodist University Press, 1989), 97–113.

13. Verhey, *Christian Art of Dying,* 192.

14. Derek Humphry, *Final Exit: The Practicalities of Self-Deliverance and Assisted Suicide,* 3rd ed. (New York: Random House, 2002).

15. Maynard, "My Right to Death with Dignity."

16. Ann Voscamp, "Dear Brittany: Why We Don't Have to Be So Afraid of Dying and Suffering That We Choose Suicide," *The Aquila Report,* October 14, 2014, http://theaquilareport.com/dear-brittany-why-we-dont-have-to-be-so-afraid-of-dying-suffering-that-we-choose-suicide/.

17. Jessica Kelley, "Can Christians Support Brittany Maynard's Decision?" October 9, 2014. Kelley's original blog post quoted here has been taken down. A much shorter statement under this same title can be found at http://www.calliegloriosomays.com/?p=1375.

18. Ibid.

19. Not Dead Yet, http://notdeadyet.org/about.

20. Gloria Maxson, "'Whose Life Is It Anyway?' Ours, That's Whose!" in *On Moral Medicine: Theological Perspectives in Medical Ethics,* 2nd ed., ed. Stephen E. Lammers and Allen Verhey (Grand Rapids: Wm. B. Eerdmans Publishing Co., 1998), 648.

21. Ibid., 649.

22. Haider Warraich, *Modern Death: How Medicine Changed the End of Life* (New York: St. Martin's Press, 2017), 20.

23. Jerome E. Bickenbach, "Disability and Life-Ending Decisions," in *Physician Assisted Suicide: Expanding the Debate,* ed. Margaret P. Battin, Rosamond Rhodes, and Anita Silvers (New York: Routledge, 1998), 124.

24. Ibid., 125.

25. Thaddeus Mason Pope and Amanda West, "Legal Briefing: Voluntarily Stopping Eating and Drinking," *Journal of Clinical Ethics* 25, no. 1 (Spring 2014): 68–80.

26. See "Case Study: A Fading Decision," *Hastings Center Report* 44, no. 3 (May–June 2014): 14.

27. Tara Culp-Ressler, "Most Doctors in the United States Now Support 'Death with Dignity Laws,'" *Think Progress*, December 2014, https://thinkprogress.org/most-doctors-in-the-united-states-now-support-death-with-dignity-laws-8888c575c2ea/.

28. Both the classic version of the Hippocratic oath, which includes this quotation, and the modern version can be found online: Peter Tyson, "The Hippocratic Oath Today," *NOVA*, March 27, 2001, http://www.pbs.org/wgbh/nova/body/hippocratic-oath-today.html.

29. Jessica Nutik Zitter, "Should I Help My Patients Die?" *New York Times*, August 5, 2017, https://www.nytimes.com/2017/08/05/opinion/sunday/dying-doctors-palliative-medicine.html.

30. *How to Die in Oregon*, directed by Peter Richardson (Cinedigm Studios, 2011), DVD.

31. Harris Meyer, "What California Providers Will Do When Asked to Help Patients Die," *Modern Healthcare*, March 11, 2016, http://www.modernhealthcare.com/article/20160311/NEWS/303129980.

32. Timothy E. Quill, "Death and Dignity—A Case of Individualized Decision Making," *New England. Journal of Medicine* 324 (1991): 691–94.

33. Anonymous, "It's Over, Debbie," *Journal of the American Medical Association* 259, no. 2 (1989): 272, doi:10.1001/jama.259.2.272.

34. Timothy C. Rowe, MB, FRCSC, FRCOG, "It's Still Not Over, Debbie," *British Columbia Medical Journal* 56, no. 8 (October 2014): 378, http://www.bcmj.org/editorials/its-still-not-over-debbie.

35. Jessica Nutik Zitter, *Extreme Measures: Finding a Better Path to the End of Life* (New York: Penguin Random House, 2017), 5.

36. See note 17 above.

Chapter 4: Physician-Patient Relations and Advance Directives

1. Atul Gawande, *Being Mortal: Medicine and What Matters in the End* (New York: Henry Holt & Co., 2014), 200.

2. Ibid., 197.

3. Paul L. Lehmann, *The Decalogue and a Human Future: The Meaning of the Commandments for Making and Keeping Human Life Human* (Grand Rapids: Wm. B. Eerdmans Publishing Co., 1995). Now available through Wipf & Stock Publishers, 2002, 37–38.

4. Gawande, *Being Mortal*, 200.

5. Ibid.

6. Lehmann, *Decalogue*, 45.

7. Gawande, *Being Mortal*, 217–18.

8. Ibid., 218.

9. Ibid., 201.

10. Ibid., 198.

11. Ibid., 199.

12. Margaret E. Mohrmann, "The Practice of the Ministry of Medicine," Loma Linda University Center for Christian Bioethics, *Update* 14, no 3, (October 1998): 1. Another version of the same essay, titled "Stories and Suffering," can be found in *On Moral Medicine, Theological Perspectives in Medical Ethics*, 2nd ed., ed. Stephen E. Lammers and Allen Verhey (Grand Rapids: Wm. B. Eerdmans Publishing Co., 1998), 347–55.

13. Ibid.

14. "History of Living Wills," Law Offices of Schlissel DeCorpo, LLP, http://www.schlissellawfirm.com/history-of-living-wills/.

15. Dee Leahman, "Why the Patient Self-Determination Act Has Failed," *North Carolina Medical Journal* 65, no. 4 (July/August 2004): 249–51.

16. Jessica Nutik Zitter, *Extreme Measures: Finding a Better Path to the End of Life* (New York: Penguin Random House, 2017), 134.

17. Allen Verhey, *The Christian Art of Dying: Learning from Jesus* (Grand Rapids: Wm. B. Eerdmans Publishing Co., 2011), 357.

18. Zitter, *Extreme Measures*, 289.

19. Ibid., 1.

20. Ibid., 135.

21. Ibid., 136.

22. Ibid., 186–92.

23. Tiffanie Win, "Why Don't More People Want to Donate Their Organs?" *The Atlantic*, November 10, 2014, https://www.theatlantic.com/health/archive/2014/11/why-dont-people-want-to-donate-their-organs/382297/.

24. "State-by-State POLST Forms," Everplans, 2018, https://www.everplans.com/articles/state-by-state-polst-forms.

25. "National POLST Paradigm Fundamentals," National POLST Paradigm, 2018, http://polst.org/about-the-national-polst-paradigm/what-is-polst/.

26. Leslie Kernisan, "POLST: Resources and Tips on Avoiding Pitfalls," in *Better Health while Aging: Practical Information for Senior Health and Family Caregivers*, 2018, http://betterhealthwhileaging.net/polst-resources-tips-avoid-pitfalls/.

27. Karen M. Wyatt, MD, "How to Have Everyday Conversations about Death and Dying," *HUFFPOST,* February 10, 2017, http://www.huffingtonpost.com/karen-m-wyatt-md/how-to-have-everyday-conversations-about-death-and-dying_b_9033040.html.

28. Jaweed Kaleem, "My Gift of Grace Card Game about Death Seeks to Spark Conversations," *HUFFPOST,* updated December 6, 2017, https://www.huffingtonpost.com/2013/07/29/my-gift-of-grace-death_n_3648832.html.

29. Richard Harris, "Discussing Death over Dinner," *The Atlantic,* April 16, 2016, https://www.theatlantic.com/health/archive/2016/04/discussing-death-over-dinner/478452/.

30. For more about this program, see http://deathoverdinner.org/.

31. American Bar Association, Commission on Law and Aging, "Toolkit for Health Care Advance Planning," http://www.americanbar.org/groups/law_aging/resources/health_care_decision_making/consumer_s_toolkit_for_health_care_advance_planning.html.

Chapter 5: Funerals, Burial, and Grief

1. Caitlin Doughty, *From Here to Eternity: Traveling the World to Find the Good Death* (New York: W. W. Norton & Co., 2017), 6.

2. *There Was a Child* (Fred Simon, Fanlight Productions, 1991) is a powerful half-hour documentary that interviews women who experienced miscarriage or stillbirth. It can still be purchased online for about $150.00 at http://www.fanlight.com/catalog/films/048_twac.php.

3. For information on how to set up a memorialized account or have your account deleted after you die, see https://www.facebook.com/help/1506822589577997.

4. See, for instance, "A Guide to Facebook Etiquette after Someone Has Died," Mashable, https://mashable.com/2017/04/08/facebook-etiquette-grief/#CF9wyjEQ0Pq5.

5. Doughty, *From Here to Eternity*, 24–25.

6. Ibid., 21.

7. Jonah Engel Bromwich, "An Alternative to Burial and Cremation Gains Popularity," *New York Times,* October 19, 2017, https://mobile.nytimes.com/2017/10/19/business/flameless-cremation.html?smid=fb-nytimes&smtyp=cur&referer=http%3A%2F%2Fm.facebook.com.

8. Caitlin Doughty, "North Carolina: Cullowhee," in Doughty, *From Here to Eternity*, 105–36.

9. Thomas G. Long, *Accompany Them with Singing: The*

Christian Funeral (Louisville, KY: Westminster John Knox Press, 2009), 33 and 35.

10. Ibid., 35.

11. *Book of Common Worship* (Louisville, KY: Westminster/John Knox Press, 1993), 917–18.

12. Elisabeth Kübler-Ross, *On Death and Dying: What the Dying Have to Teach Doctors, Nurses, Clergy and Their Own Families*, 40th anniversary ed. (New York: Routledge, Taylor, and Frances Group, 2009).

13. K. A. Leddy, "Ducking Grief," *New York Times*, October 22, 2013, http://www.nytimes.com/2013/10/22/booming/ducking-grief.html.

14. Patrick O'Malley, "Getting Grief Right," *New York Times*, January 10, 2015, https://opinionator.blogs.nytimes.com/2015/01/10/getting -grief-right/.

15. Ibid.

16. Stanley Hauerwas, *Suffering Presence: Theological Reflections on Medicine, the Mentally Handicapped, and the Church* (Notre Dame, IN: University of Notre Dame Press, 1986).

17. Nicholas Wolterstorff, *Lament for a Son* (Grand Rapids: Wm. B. Eerdmans Publishing Co., 1987), 31.

18. *The Constitution of the Presbyterian Church (U.S.A.),* Part I, *Book of Confessions* (Louisville, KY: Office of the General Assembly, Presbyterian Church (U.S.A.), 2016), 4.001.

CPSIA information can be obtained
at www.ICGtesting.com
Printed in the USA
FSHW02n2221230818
51510FS